Connecticut

in the GOLDEN AGE *of*

SPIRITUALISM

October 5, 2016

To Terri,

Hope you enjoy learning more about D. D Home and are inspired by her mediumship

With Blessings,
Elaine Kuzmeskus

Connecticut

in the GOLDEN AGE of
SPIRITUALISM

ELAINE M. KUZMESKUS

THE
History
PRESS

Published by The History Press
Charleston, SC
www.historypress.net

First published 2016

Manufactured in the United States

ISBN 978.1.46711.841.5

Library of Congress Control Number: 2016938318

This book is dedicated to the memory of Reverend Dorothy Smith,
Reverend Carl Hewitt and Reverend Calista Rita.
These Connecticut mediums demonstrated the first tenet of Spiritualism:
"There is no death and there are no dead."

CONTENTS

ACKNOWLEDGEMENTS

Putting a book together requires a great deal of time, effort and patience from the author, researchers, editors and publisher. My task was made easier by the kind assistance of several individuals. I would like to express my gratitude to Dr. Susan Roberts for editing the initial text. Her knowledge of English and sensitivity to the occult subject matter made her the perfect choice for the book. I also wish to thank Elizabeth Burgess of the Stowe Center, Tracy Brindle and Mallory Howard of the Mark Twain House, Melanie Bourbeau of the Hill-Stead Museum and the staff of the Connecticut Historical Society for their assistance with research. A special thanks goes to Steve Blais for the many hours he spent formatting the images. Finally, I would like to thank Tabitha Dulla; Karmen Cook, acquisitions editor with The History Press; and Abigail Fleming, production editor with The History Press, for their input. While Tabitha encouraged me to write the book, Karmen patiently guided me throughout the process of getting the book to print and Abigail skillfully edited and polished the final version of *Connecticut in the Golden Age of Spiritualism*.

Introduction

CONNECTICUT MEDIUMS

Believe that life is worth living and your belief will create the fact.
—Professor William James

I began my journey into Spiritualism in the summer of 1969 when I visited the First Spiritualist Church of Onset, Massachusetts. There I received evidential messages from the church's pastors, Reverend Kenneth and Gladys Custance. Two years later, while I was training to be a medium myself, I spent a summer as a guest in the parish house of the church.

It turned out to be a good opportunity to observe a variety of fine mediums. One, Reverend Gertrude McCauley, predicted that I would move to Connecticut. At the time, I doubted I would ever leave Boston, as the city was the hub of my universe. I filled my days with yoga classes, astrology lessons and the Friday night development circle led by Mrs. Custance. However, Reverend McCauley persisted: "I see Connecticut over your head. You are going to Connecticut." Less than two years later, her prophecy came true when I married Ronald Kuzmeskus, who worked in the "Constitution State." We happily moved to Suffield, Connecticut, where we have lived for the past forty years.

While staying in Onset, I had the opportunity to observe a veteran Connecticut medium, Reverend Calista Rita, the pastor of the Norwich Spiritualist church. As a fledging medium, I was in awe of the short older lady who sported a bouffant hairdo. I loved to listen to her and her companion Mrs. Russell as they chain-smoked and bantered in the backyard. When I asked Reverend Rita how she became a medium, she told me that she was born with the gift of clairvoyance and saw spirit people as a child in Norwich, Connecticut. Terrified, she kept this knowledge to herself. Finally, unable to keep the secret bottled up any longer, she told her Portuguese mother. A good Catholic, her mother was appalled but loved her daughter enough to listen. Her spirit guides came to the child's rescue and put Calista into a trance. While the young girl was taken over by spirit, her deceased relatives came through with messages so authentic her mother never doubted her daughter's mediumship again.

Later, as an adult, Calista Rita joined a development circle led by Matilda Russell, who became a lifelong friend. When Reverend Rita preached, the congregation never knew who the speaker would be, as she always delivered her sermon deep in trance with her eyes closed. She transformed in front of our eyes from a motherly woman to an erudite speaker with the mannerisms and deeper voice of an authoritarian male.

By the time I moved to Connecticut, I was a medium certified by the National Association of Spiritualist Churches. When my husband became interested in learning about mediumship and healing, I suggested that he take classes with Reverend Carl Hewitt in Chesterfield, Connecticut. The medium bore an uncanny resemblance to President Jimmy Carter, and with his soft southern accent, he sounded a bit like Carter as well. Reverend Hewitt was not a trance medium but a superb mental medium—one who contacts spirits through clairsentience (feeling the spirit), clairaudience (hearing the spirit) or clairvoyance (seeing the spirit). When he became interested in studying physical phenomena (table tipping, direct voice and spirit materialization), he had a séance room constructed in the basement of his ranch-style home. To be sure that the room was totally dark, as required for phenomena, he chose a room without windows and painted the walls black.

I was only able to attend the first class with Ron, but I am glad I did. After joining hands in prayer, Carl put on a meditation tape that had the soothing sounds of nature. When he turned on the lights on after our forty-minute meditation, I surprised by the sight of my husband's ashen face. "What is wrong?" I said softly. Ron could barely speak. He only managed to whisper, "I'll tell you later." On the ride home, he told me how as soon as Carl put on the music, he had left his body and could not get back in until the cassette tape stopped. Apparently, Ron spent the meditation floating on the ceiling of the séance room.

Another Connecticut medium who made an impression on us was Reverend Dorothy Smith. She and her husband, Reverend Melvin Smith, served as pastors for the Albertson Memorial Church in Old Greenwich, Connecticut. The church was founded by Stamford chiropractor Dr. Isabelle MacDonald in 1936. She started the organization with a small prayer group in her home for people who wished to develop their gifts of the spirit. When the group decided to start a church, the doctor named it after her spirit guide, Dr. Albertson.

Dorothy Smith joined MacDonald's circle when she moved to Stamford. The British Spiritualist was a welcome addition to the group. She was a lovely woman with well-coiffed brunette hair and always fashionably attired. With her clipped British accent, she appeared the perfect lady, which was an asset in her job as a real estate broker. Few of her clients realized that under her traditional façade dwelt a brilliant Spiritualist medium.

Every year, from 1988 until her death in 2004, we scheduled an annual reading with Reverend Smith. She was always compassionate and correctly tuned in to loved ones and guides. The medium was also uncannily accurate in her predictions. For instance, Dorothy told me once in a reading that my teenage son Adam would be a doctor, and Heather, our daughter, would be a lawyer. Both prophecies came true even though I never told her predictions to the children.

By the time Dorothy Smith had passed to spirit, I had just started researching *Connecticut Ghosts*. Occasionally, I could her feel her presence as I sought to prove the existence of spirits in various locations throughout the state. While doing research for my second book on mediumship, *Séance 101: Physical Mediumship*, I came across the name of Daniel Dunglas Home, the subject of chapter 5. He was one of the few physical mediums who could tip tables, levitate and give exceptional trance demonstrations.

In the Victorian era, physical demonstrations of mediumship such as table tipping and the use of a planchette for automatic writing were popular. Prominent citizens such as Harriet Beecher Stowe and her half-sister, Isabella Beecher Hooker, held séances in their Hartford homes. They were not the only members of the famous Beecher family interested in spiritualism. Their brother Charles Beecher wrote an expensive description of spirit communication in his book *Spiritual Manifestations*. He even gave credence to the case of the Stratford Poltergeist.

Other Connecticut residents who contributed to the heyday of Spiritualism include Reverend Andrew Jackson Davis, who lived in Hartford from 1850 to 1854; Nettie Colburn Maynard, who conducted séances at the White House; and Theodate Pope Riddle, a survivor of the *Lusitania*, who used her fortune to further the parapsychology research of William James. As a psychologist and the author of *Varieties of Religious Experiences*, James was a serious student of mediumship. He believed it was possible to communicate with the other side. He also noted the importance of a positive attitude. William James is quoted as saying, "Believe that life is worth living and your belief will create the fact." Spiritualists, of course, would insist that life is *continuously* worth living.

1
INFLUENCES ON
CONNECTICUT SPIRITUALISTS

We affirm that the existence and personal identity of the individual continue after the change called death.
—*Declaration of Principles, National Spiritualist Association of Churches*

Connecticut Spiritualists believe that individuals continue to exist after death and that communication with the dead was indeed possible. This belief in life after death is not new. It has been a topic of fascination since the days of ancient Egypt, when the pharaohs made elaborate preparation for the afterlife. The early Greeks also believed in an afterlife, which they called Elysian Fields, and held their oracles in high esteem.

The most famous of the Greek seers was the oracle at Delphi. Heads of state, military generals and emperors sought her council. When the Roman emperor Nero consulted her, she cried out, "Your presence defies me. Be gone matricide, beware of seventy-three!" At the time, Nero took the prophecy to mean he would die at seventy-three. The thirty-year-old emperor was relieved to know he had another forty-three years to live. However, he was incorrect in his assumption, as he died the next year. Seventy-three-year-old Galba succeeded him.[1]

Although belief in spirits goes back for thousands of years, colonists in Connecticut denounced communication with the dead as witchcraft, a crime punishable by death. However, in Europe two enlightened thinkers emerged: Emanuel Swedenborg (1688–1772) and Franz Anton Mesmer (1734–1815). While Swedenborg communicated with spirits while awake, and described higher and lower heavens and hells, Mesmer was not attracted to religion. He was more interested in healing and developed a method of trance to assist his patients.

Early mediums such as Andrew Jackson Davis utilized hypnotism to go into a trance. Davis was a medium, faith healer and prophet. He began his career in Hartford, where he honed his skill as medical clairvoyant and channeler. Davis even predicted the birth of Spiritualism in his book *Principles of Nature*, first published in 1847:

> *It is a truth that spirits commune with one another while one is in the body and the other in the higher spheres—and this, too, when the person in the body is unconscious of the influx, and hence cannot be convinced of the fact; and this truth will ere long present itself in the form of a living demonstration. And the world will hail with delight the ushering in of that era when the interiors of men will be opened, and the spiritual communion will be established.*[2]

The next year, on March 31, 1848, two young sisters, Katherine "Kate" and Margaret "Maggie" Fox, of Hydesville, New York, established spirit communication with a deceased peddler, whom they dubbed "Mr. Splitfoot." Kate decided to ask the spirit questions. "Mr. Splitfoot obliged by giving one rap for yes and no rap meant no. Their mother even tested the spirit by asking Mr. Splitfoot to rap out the ages of her children. It did so correctly even including a child that had died in infancy."[3]

The girls soon became well known for their table tipping and spirit raps. They devised a method of communicating though raps by using the number of raps to tap out the letters of the alphabet. Slowly, spirits loudly rapped out a message, which encouraged the girls to spread the truth of spirit communication: "Dear friends, you must proclaim this truth to the world. This is the dawning of a new era; you must not try to conceal it any longer. When you do your duty God will protect you and good spirits will watch over you."[4]

The family followed the spirit's advice. On November 14, 1849, Maggie and Kate were put on stage at the Corinthian Hall in Rochester to demonstrate spirit raps. Naturally there were skeptics present, but the girls passed inspection of three committees: "The spirits came through and made the usual physical manifestations. Also, a challenge was made; a committee from the audience would be selected by the audience to examine the mediums and the manifestations to determine if they be genuine; the committee was to give its report the following evening. After investigation, the committee was convinced of the genuiness [*sic*] of the mediums and the phenomena. Two more committees were subsequently selected and reached the same conclusion."[5]

The young mediums could not help but impress the audience with their table tipping and raps that accurately answered questions from the audience. Later, they used a planchette to point to the letters on a "talking board." Harriet Beecher Stowe and her half-sister, Isabella Beecher Hooker, would also adopt this method to talk to spirits.

Many of the early Victorian mediums, such as Kate and Maggie Fox and Cora L.V. Scott, performed on stage. Audiences were as enthralled with their beauty as much as with their supernatural talents. Cora was born in 1840 in the hamlet of Cuba, New York. She was born with a caul over her face, a membrane "veil" that superstitious villagers took to be a sign of supernatural powers.[6] She proved the myth to have some credence. In 1852, Cora first exhibited her ability to fall into a trance. In this state, she spoke in a voice unlike her own and even wrote messages uncharacteristic of her own script. It was not long before her impoverished parents started to put their psychic daughter on stage.[7] "By the age of 15, she was making public appearances in which she spoke with 'supernatural eloquence' on almost any topic put forward by the audience, all while claiming to be in a trance. Contemporary audiences found the spectacle itself incredible: a very young and pretty girl declaiming with authority on esoteric subjects; it was enough to convince many people that she was indeed a channel for spirits."[8]

Eventually, she became one of the leading trance lecturers of the Spiritualist movement and delivered discourses on the other side of life to large audiences. For example, on May 10, 1874, Cora L.V. Tappan delivered a trance philosophical talk at Cleveland Hall in London. The following week, the spirit of Judge John W. Edmonds, who had died two months earlier, came through Mrs. Tappan to deliver an address to the audience in Cleveland Hall.

She married four times and worked under the last names of her husbands: Hatch, Daniels, Tappan and Richmond. When she returned to the United States in 1875, she took the position of pastor of a Spiritualist church in Chicago. In 1893, she delivered a presentation on Spiritualism at the Parliament of the World's Religions in Chicago.[7] She was also instrumental in founding the National Spiritualist Association and served as its first vice president.

Not all mediums were involved in national organizations. William and Horatio Eddy had no interest whatsoever in the burgeoning Spiritualist community. Growing up on a small farm near Chittenden, Vermont, both brothers took up mediumship as a trade. William worked in a séance cabinet with his brother Horatio as cabinet attendant. When enough ectoplasm had been extruded from the medium, the first spirit would emerge from the cabinet. The Eddy brothers were able to produce full-bodied materialization of spirits of American Indians, deceased relatives and guides. "The spirits ranged in size from over six feet to very small (it's worth noting here that William Eddy was only five feet, nine inches tall)."[10]

Some of the forms were transparent, while others appeared solid, like a spirit that greeted Helena Blavatsky. She described a full apparition of "a tall, swarthy man who was costumed in velvet, decorated with gold braid, bedecked with tassels, and wearing high leather boots" who saluted her before disappearing into the mist.[11] This and other astounding materializations are detailed in Henry Steel Olcott's book *People from the Other World*.

While the Eddy brothers' mediumship was deemed genuine by Olcott, he was disappointed in Eliza "Lizzie" White. He disclosed, "I am sorry to say that investigation into personal history of this woman discloses little to her credit." Lizzie, who hailed from Winsted, Connecticut, worked in conjunction with two well-known Philadelphia mediums, Mr. and Mrs. Nelson Holmes. She met them when the couple stayed at her boardinghouse in March 1874. For eight months, the trio put on spectacular séances in which the "spirit" of Katie King would materialize in the séance room. The audience gasped as they saw the lovely young spirit shrouded in white emerge from the spirit cabinet. Soon, everyone wanted to attend their séances, including Vice President Henry Wilson.

Nelson and Jennie Holmes made quite an impression on psychic investigators such as Robert Dale Owen. He wrote this endorsement for the *Galaxy* in December 1874:

I have seen Katie on seven or eight different occasions, suspended, in full form, about two feet from the ground for ten or fifteen seconds. It was within the cabinet, but in full view; and she moved her arms and feet gently, as a swimmer upright in the water might. I have seen her, on five different evenings, disappear and reappear before my eyes, and not more than eight or nine feet distant. On one occasion, when I had given her a calla lily, she gradually vanished, holding it in her hand; and the lily remained visible after the hand which held it was gone; the flower, however, finally disappearing also. When she reappeared the lily came back also, at first a bright spot only, which gradually expanded into a flower.[12]

Owen had to withdraw his support a few weeks later when Eliza White admitted that she had impersonated Katie King by slipping in through a false panel of the cabinet.[13]

Other fraudulent mediums, such as Francis Ward Monck, preferred the stage, where large audiences were willing to pay for chicanery. In one of his séances, Monck claimed that the spirit would play a musical clock placed on a table and covered with a cigar box. In order to produce music, Monck hid a small music box in his pants.[14] He even achieved spirit materialization with the help of well-placed cheesecloth: "On November 3, 1876 during the séance a sitter demanded that Monck be searched. Monck ran from the room, locked himself in another room and escaped out of a window. A pair of stuffed gloves was found in his room, as well as cheesecloth, reaching rods and other fraudulent devices in his luggage. After a trial, Monck was convicted for his fraudulent mediumship and sentenced to three months in prison."[15]

Other mediums were exposed as frauds. In 1906, medium Charles Eldred also tried to fake materialization of spirits. In order to do so, he had a secret compartment in his chair full of paraphernalia to fake materializations. Later, in 1910, investigators discovered medium Charles Bailey, who claimed to have the ability to apport objects, including live birds, to be a fake. Apparently, he was seen purchasing his apports, two birds, prior to the séance. Finally, sympathetic scientist Dr. Schrenck-Notzing was shocked by Ladislas Lasslo's confession of fraud. According to the medium's own admission, all his materializations were produced with the assistance of a sitter who was found to be the medium's confederate.[16]

CONNECTICUT IN THE GOLDEN AGE OF SPIRITUALISM

The phenomena of Spiritualism need not further proof. They are proved, quite as well as any facts are proved in other science
—Professor Alfred Russel Wallace

The Golden Age of Spiritualism spanned from the 1850s to the 1920s. At its peak in 1897, eight million people in the United States and Europe believed that communication with the spirits of the deceased was possible.[1] Its most famous enthusiast was Mary Todd Lincoln. After the death of her beloved son Willie, she she invited medium Nettie Colburn to the White House. The young Hartford medium conducted many séances for Mary Todd Lincoln and President Lincoln. She later detailed these experiences in her book *Was Abraham Lincoln a Spiritualist?*.

Spiritualism has many aspects. It is a philosophy of life, a science and a religion. While Mrs. Lincoln believed in the philosophy of Spiritualism, she did not belong to this new offshoot of Christianity. Most Spiritualists believe in communication with the "so-called dead," and they like to consider Spiritualism a scientific religion. They prefer to believe in Infinite Intelligence rather than a patriarchal God.

Spiritualism began in Upstate New York when sisters Maggie, fifteen, and Kate Fox, twelve, heard raps in the basement of their Hydesville, New York cottage. They were delighted to discover when they clapped their hands, the spirit present would respond to their claps by making an equal number of raps. Soon they progressed to using their alphabet system of communicating with raps. They demonstrated this to neighbors, and eventually a system was worked out through which a spirit could communicate. Then they used the number of raps to tap out the letters of the alphabet. For example, one rap would be the letter *A*, two raps meant *B* and so on to twenty-six raps for *Z*. By using this method, the girls were able to receive messages from the spirit of Charles B. Rosna. The restless spirit claimed he had been murdered in the house by the former owner five years earlier. Later, human remains were found in the basement, thus confirming the story.

As soon as their story came out, the local media could talk of nothing else. Wherever the girls went, they were able to produce spirit raps. Many, including a Quaker couple, Isaac and Amy Post, believed the girls to be genuine mediums. Both Amy Post and her husband, Isaac, developed automatic writing. His 1852 book *Voices from the Spirit World, Being Communications from Many Spirits*, was dictated by spirits such as Benjamin Franklin and George Fox.

Interest in Spiritualism was at a fever pitch. Everyone wanted to see the young mediums. Horace Greeley, editor of the *New York Tribune*, sponsored séances in New York. He was convinced of their integrity. Kate Fox even lived with Greeley and his family in New York City while she completed her education. Greeley opened columns in his newspaper for anyone who wished to express spirit communication.

There was a downside to the Fox sisters' popularity. The young mediums were often taxed to the limits of their abilities. Emma Hardinge Britten, noted Spiritualist author and founder of *Two Worlds* magazine, described the teenage mediums "repeating hour after hour the letters of the alphabet, while the no less poor, patient spirits rapped out names, ages and dates to suit all comers."[2] They soon became famous mediums, hosting séances for hundreds of people who asked questions regarding "the state of railway stocks or the issue of love affairs."[3] While Horace Greeley became their protector, he was unable to entirely shield the girls, who began to drink wine. Later in life, Kate and Maggie eventually succumbed to alcoholism.

Many early Spiritualists favored women's rights, and they were sympathetic to the plight of the Fox sisters. Amy Post was a personal friend of Kate and Maggie Fox and a friend of Susan B. Anthony, who summered at Lily Dale Assembly: "Susan B. Anthony, the grand lady of the Woman's Suffrage movement, made her first public appearance at Lily Dale in 1891. So emotion filled was the event at Lily Dale, that Miss Anthony herself wrote about that special first day: 'Every cottage in the camp was festooned with yellow, and when at night the Chinese lanterns were lighted on the plazas, it was gorgeous as any Fourth of July celebration, and all in honor of Woman's Day and her coming freedom.'"[4]

In addition to Susan B. Anthony, many other prominent Americans championed Spiritualism, including New York Supreme Court justice John W. Edmonds. When circumstances forced Edmonds to choose between Spiritualism and the Supreme Court, he chose Spiritualism. When he was ridiculed by a Washington, D.C. newspaper, the *National Intelligencer*, Nathaniel Tallmadge came to his defense. The former senator described Judge Edmonds as a man of "unimpeachable integrity." In 1854, Tallmadge even presented a petition with thirteen thousand names to Congress in support of investigation into the possibility of communication with the dead:

> *Letter from Ex-Senator Tallmadge.*
> *From the* Nat. Intelligencer *of April 19.*
>
> *Messrs. Gales & Seaton: My attention has been attracted to the proceedings of the Senate, published in the Intelligencer of this morning, on the presentation of a memorial by General Shields, signed by myself and thirteen thousand citizens of the United States, on the subject of "spiritual manifestations."*[5]

While Congress did not take Tallmadge's request seriously, several eminent scientists gave communication with the so-called dead serious thought; among them was Alfred Russel Wallace, the British naturalist and explorer, who began investigating Spiritualism in the summer of 1865. After witnessing several séances, he was convinced that séance phenomena was real. Other prominent nineteenth-century intellectuals involved with Spiritualism were the social reformer Robert Owen, physicist William Crookes and noted novelist Victor Hugo.

Hugo turned to Spiritualism while he was in political exile on the Channel Island of Jersey in the English Channel. He formed a circle to experiment with table tipping and then used mediums to communicate with the other side. The group made contact with a spirit identifying himself as Martin Luther. When Victor Hugo asked why God does not better reveal himself, the spirit of the Father of the Protestant Reformation replied, "Because doubt is the instrument which forges the human spirit. If the day were to come when the human spirit no longer doubted, the human soul would fly off and leave the plough behind, for it would have acquired wings. The earth would lie fallow. Now, God is the sower and man the harvester. The celestial seed demands that the human ploughshare remain in the furrow of life."[6]

Several other Victorians wrote books on Spiritualism. Professor J.S. Loveland, a former Methodist minister, wrote one of the first American books on Spiritualism: *Esoteric Truths of Spiritualism*. Later, Dr. James Martin Peebles published *Spiritualism through the Ages* in 1869. The book examines the history of religion and spirituality and spirit communication. The author was a physician and a minister as well as a Spiritualist and Theosophist. One of Peebles's most popular books was *How to Live a Century and Grow Old Gracefully*. Peebles, born March 23, 1822, died on February 15, 1922—one month short of his 100th birthday.

Another Spiritualist writer, Hudson Tuttle, defined the tenets of mediumship in his book *The Arcana of Nature and Mediumship and Its Laws*. The devout Ohio Spiritualist wrote several books on Spiritualism. He even formed his own publishing company from his Ohio home. Tuttle, who had only had a year of formal education, always gave credit to spirit communicators for his writing. Later, he invented a dial plate with an alphabet, numbers zero through nine and phrases he "psychographed." The frontispiece is printed with an intricate square border around a circular dial that reads "Yes," "No," "Good Bye" and "Don't Know." Tuttle gave these instructions for its use: "The instrument is not a mere machine that will grind out communications; it is only a delicate means. It must be used intelligently. The sitter should sit with reverent seriousness, and undivided desire, and at fixed times, and not become discouraged if many sittings pass without results." The Psychograph became popular on both sides of the Atlantic.[7]

Spiritualist practices were popular in Connecticut as well. Two years later, in March 1850, spirit communication arrived in Connecticut in the most peculiar manner. The spirits caused quite a ruckus in Stratford, Connecticut. Reverend Eliakim Phelps, a Congregational minister, was shocked to see objects began to move about the house. "An umbrella jumped into the air and traveled nearly 25 feet . . . forks, spoons, knives, books, pens and assorted small objects launched from places where no one had been standing . . . pillows, sheets and blankets were pulled from beds and fluttered into the air. This continued all day long and finally, by evening, the activity seemed to be exhausted and the house fell silent."[8] It was not long before everyone in Stratford heard about hauntings at the Phelps home. Some believed the hauntings were connected to the death of Goody Bassett, who was hanged as a witch near the Elm Street mansion.

Over a period of six months, the family witnessed Reverend Phelps's son being carried across a room by invisible hands and family members being pinched and slapped by unseen forces. The family was terrorized by objects moving through the air, furniture overturning on its own and the sound of shattered glass as windows broke. The most disturbing phenomenon was mysterious noises sounding at all hours. The loud rappings, knockings and poundings kept people awake at night and on edge during the day.[9] Reverend Jackson Davis, who had an office in Connecticut, was called in to investigate. He "asserted his belief in the genuineness of the activity."[10]

Reverend Andrew Jackson Davis's opinion was taken seriously. He contributed much to Spiritualism, as did Robert Dale Owen, who was famous for introducing the bill that organized the Smithsonian Institution. Owen was also the Spiritualist who researched New London medium Daniel Dunglas Home, who was regarded as the greatest physical medium in modern Spiritualism. Home demonstrated trance and materialization along with levitation.

Spiritualism caused quite stir in Hartford as well. Its most famous citizen, Mark Twain, liked to poke fun at séances. After attending one in 1866, he made this tongue-in-cheek comment: "I got hold of the right Smith at last—the particular Smith I was after—my dear, lost, lamented friend—and learned that he died a violent death. I feared as much. He said his wife talked him to death. Poor wretch!"[11]

While Mark Twain did not take mediums too seriously, other Nook Farm residents embraced Spiritualism. Both Harriet Beecher Stowe and her half-sister, Isabella Beecher Hooker, were passionate about abolition, women's rights and Spiritualism. They both attended séances here and abroad. The Stowes were drawn to Spiritualism after the tragic death their son Henry, who was studying at Dartmouth College in Hanover, New Hampshire. The young man died at nineteen in a swimming accident while at home on vacation. Harriet's half-sister, Isabella, also explored Spiritualism and held séances to reach departed family and friends. She and her husband, John Hooker, a descendant of Hartford's founding father, Thomas Hooker, were enthusiastic about Spiritualism. Later in life, she developed her own mediumship and even had séances with her granddaughter Katherine Seymour Day.

Isabella was a firm believer in women's rights. Many other suffragettes were fascinated by Spiritualism, including Victoria Woodhull, the first female candidate for the presidency. She ran in 1872 on the Equal Rights Party ticket. She was also a magnetic healer and medium. She certainly stirred up the citizens of Hartford when she published an account of the alleged adulterous affair between the prominent minister Henry Ward Beecher and his parishioner Elizabeth Tilton. When Victoria Woodhull came to Hartford soon after the incident, Mark Twain dubbed her "Mrs. Satan."

Above: Connecticut state capitol. *Wikimedia Commons.*

Right: A daguerreotype portrait by T.M. Easterly of Kate and Maggie Fox, 1852. *Missouri History Museum.*

As the Golden Age of Spiritualism came to a close, science began to take note of the investigation into the possibility of life after death. One very generous Connecticut dame, Theodate Pope Riddle, supported research at Harvard University. She was also a major figure in the American Society for Psychical Research. While her dream of establishing a society for psychic research in Connecticut did not come to fruition, she did host some lively séances at her Farmington home.

ANDREW JACKSON DAVIS IN HARTFORD

Under all circumstances, keep an even mind.[1]
—*Andrew Jackson Davis*

Andrew Jackson Davis is frequently referred to as the John the Baptist of Spiritualism—for good reason. On March 31, 1848, the very day the Fox sisters began hearing raps in their basement, Davis wrote in his diary, "About daylight this morning a warm breathing passed over my face and I heard a voice, tender and strong, saying, 'Brother, the good work has begun—behold, a living demonstration is born.' I was left wondering what could be meant by such a message."[2]

Not only did Andrew Jackson Davis announce the arrival of modern Spiritualism, but he also contributed much to Spiritualism in Connecticut. From 1850 to 1854, he maintained an office in Hartford, Connecticut. He was not in Hartford long before he became known as an extraordinary trance medium. He received communication from spirits in much the same manner as ancient Greek oracles received information from the god Apollo. In Davis's case, his guide was not Apollo but the spirit of the Greek physician Marcus Galen and the spirit of Swedish seer Emanuel Swedenborg.

Andrew Jackson Davis was born in Orange County, New York, on August 11, 1826, to a ne'er-do-well father prone to bouts with alcohol. Sadly, his father earned only a meager living as a weaver and shoemaker.[3] Most of what he earned went to rum rather than food for the family. Davis's mother, however, was quite mystical, though largely illiterate. At best, she could recognize a few words from the Bible.

Apparently, Davis inherited his mother's spiritual tendencies, as he was given to mystical experiences early in life. As a child, Davis often heard spirit voices that sought to advise him. He was not only a natural clairaudient but a clairvoyant as well. For instance, "Upon his Mother's passing he saw a beautiful home in the brightness and he knew that was where his Mother went. Years later he coined the phrase 'Summerland' to describe his vision of 'Heaven.'"[4]

One particularly vivid vision on the evening of March 6, 1844, changed the course of his life. Davis experienced what Spiritualists term "traveling clairvoyance" and what parapsychologists now term "remote viewing." This faculty of seeing events and places at a distance has been used by shamans in Tibet, India and North and South America. Jesuit missionaries gave accounts of traveling clairvoyance among the Indians: "After going into trance, a shaman often could describe an approaching party of white explorers and when, after two or three days, the party finally arrived would tell them exactly which way they had come and where they had camped, and describe incidents that had occurred during the trip."[5]

While he was in this out-of-body state, Andrew Jackson Davis traveled clairvoyantly to mountains some forty miles away. Here, he made contact with master guides—Marcus Galen and seer Emanuel Swedenborg. Galen delivered a discourse on the healing power of nature and provided a magic staff with strips with cures for diseases. Then Swedenborg stepped forward to give his discourse, which ended with the prophecy that Davis would become "an appropriate vessel for the influx and perception of truth and wisdom."[6]

A few days later, while in a mesmerized state, Davis saw the glowing image of Galen's staff. It vanished, and words appeared. Davis peacefully read the message:

> *Behold!*
> *Here is thy Magic Staff.*
> *Under all Circumstances, Keep an Even Mind.*
> *Take it, Try it, Walk with it.*
> *Talk with it, Lean on it, Believe in it.*
> *For Ever* [7]

Davis took the advice of spirit and became a full trance medium, well known for his medical clairvoyance. While in a state of trance, the young medium was able to accurately diagnose medical disorders. Davis described how he could see clairvoyantly into the human body: "Each organ stood out clearly with a special luminosity of its own which greatly diminished in cases of disease."[8]

Andrew Jackson Davis quickly drew the attention of those in dire straits. He not only attended patients in his hometown of Poughkeepsie but also traveled to several other cities in Connecticut to treat the ill. Two times a day, Davis went into trance in order diagnose and prescribe treatment. At first, Davis required the services of a hypnotist to go into trance. At the start of his career, a local tailor named William Levingston hypnotized Davis. Later, Davis worked with New Haven doctor and magnetizer Dr. Silas Lyon, whom he convinced to become his personal hypnotist. Three months later, Davis asked William Fishbough, a New Haven Universalist minister, to become his private scribe. According to Fishbough, it would take Dr. Lyons three or four minutes to induce trance. When the process was complete, Davis would go into a convulsive shock. "For four or five minutes, he would remain silent and motionless, although occasional convulsive movements of his body might occur. He would then become cataleptic—his body cold, rigid, insensible, his pulse feeble, and his breathing apparently suspended."[9]

A spirit guide would then enter Davis's sleeping body, and Fishbough was right there to write down Davis's words, verbatim. "For fifteen months Dr. Lyon, his magnetizer, repeated each sentence as he uttered it, and the Rev. Fishbough, the scribe, took them down, restricting himself to grammatical corrections only."[10] The series of lectures resulted in a seven-hundred-page book, *The Principles of Nature, Her Divine Revelations, and a Voice to Mankind*. In its pages, spirits explained to readers that "the Divine Mind is the Cause, the Universe is the Effect, and Spirit is the ultimate Design."[11]

While Davis attracted very high spirits of Galen and Swedenborg, he knew there were also mischievous spirits on the other side. He warned readers to use discernment: "All spirits are not wise, pure, and holy beings. There are untruthful, ignorant, immoral, selfish, impure, and un-spiritual spirits."[12]

When Andrew Jackson Davis lived in his Hartford cottage, he devoted his time to channeling. He began *The Great Harmonia* in spartan quarters of the Charter Oak home. The five-volume work took eight years to complete. From 1850 to 1858, he brought through channeled material on health and disease, psychology, clairvoyance, social reform and marriage. Eventually, the young man with no formal education channeled information on the formation of the solar system, the geological formation of the earth, the principles of prophecy and a detailed history of the Old Testament.

Davis was also instrumental in organizing the Harmonial Brotherhood, which began on May 4, 1851, in Hartford, Connecticut. Its motto was "Universal Liberty, Fraternity, and Unity," and the group declared the following:

> *We conclude our Declaration of Independence, by affirming—what we do most religiously believe—that all men to be heaven-worthy must aspire to heaven; to be perfect; they must aspire to perfection. But this no man can perfectly do of himself; because man necessarily depends upon the favorableness of progenitary bias; upon the propitiousness of outer conditions; and upon the harmoniousness of social circumstances, for his opportunity and ability to practice such aspiration! And yet, harmony must begin with the Individual; it will thence spread over our families and communities; then it will flow and ramify through the innumerable veins and arteries of the distant sects and nations; then the Whole will represent the Individual! the Individual the Whole; and God will be all in all!!!*[13]

In his day, Davis's views on universal brotherhood and marriage, as well as his descriptions of the afterlife, were considered radical. Quite simply, he believed in the "marriage of true minds." His ideas on marriage were unusual for Victorian times. Such views were shared by Catherine DeWolfe Dodge, a wealthy woman trapped in a loveless marriage to Joshua Dodge. Her husband had served as American consul in Marseilles, France. However successful her husband, Mrs. Dodge was smitten with the youthful medium. She was so impressed that she removed a valuable ring from her finger and insisted on giving it to Davis. She also gave him $1,000 to publish his book and advanced another $1,200 to cover expenses in England. Still seeking to court Davis's favor, she gave him a house she had purchased in Waltham, Massachusetts, which Davis turned down. However, he was willing to accept her offer of an apartment. Within eighteen months, Andrew Jackson Davis proposed to the wealthy woman twenty years his senior. She accepted the offer and promptly divorced her husband.[14] The marriage, which took place on July 1, 1848, lasted until Catherine's death in 1853. He referred to his first wife as his "spiritual sister."

Two years later, Davis married another divorcée, Mary Fenn Love. The second Mrs. Davis was both a Spiritualist and a feminist. However, after thirty years of marriage, Andrew Jackson Davis claimed he and Mary were no longer soul mates. Mary Davis did not contest the divorce and distanced herself from her former husband by taking her mother's maiden name, Fenn.

Davis moved quickly to marry a much younger woman, Della E. Markham, in 1885. Davis met Della while attending medical school. At the age of sixty, the medical clairvoyant received a degree from the United States Medical College in New York. Andrew Jackson Davis then moved to Boston to practice medicine. He also ran a small bookstore where he sold books as well as herbal remedies to his patients. Davis made his transition to spirit on January 13, 1910.

He left a legacy of over thirty books in forty-five editions. In the *Penetralia*, written in 1856, Davis described the automobile a good twenty years before German inventor Karl Benz built the first car: "Look out about these days for carriages and travelling saloons on country roads—without horses, without steam, without any visible motive power—moving with greater speed and far more safety than at present. Carriages will be moved by a strange and beautiful and simple admixture of aqueous and atmospheric gases—so easily

Andrew Jackson Davis, American Spiritualist, 1847. *Wikimedia Commons.*

THE

PRINCIPLES OF NATURE,

HER DIVINE REVELATIONS,

AND

A VOICE TO MANKIND.

BY AND THROUGH

ANDREW JACKSON DAVIS,
THE "POUGHKEEPSIE SEER" AND "CLAIRVOYANT."

IN THREE PARTS.

PART FIRST.

Any theory, hypothesis, philosophy, sect, creed, or institution, that fears investigation, openly manifests its own error.

PART SECOND.

Reason is a flower of the spirit, and its fragrance is liberty and knowledge.

PART THIRD.

When distributive justice pervades the social world, virtue and morality will bloom with an immortal beauty ; while the Sun of Righteousness will arise in the horizon of universal industry, and shed its genial rays over all the fields of peace, plenty, and HUMAN HAPPINESS!

THIRD EDITION.

NEW YORK:
PUBLISHED BY S. S. LYON, AND WM. FISHBOUGH.
FOR SALE, WHOLESALE AND RETAIL, BY J. S. REDFIELD, CLINTON HALL.

1847.

The Magic Staff, autobiography of Reverend Andrew Jackson Davis. *Cornell University Library.*

condensed, so simply ignited, and so imparted by a machine somewhat resembling fire engines as to be entirely concealed and manageable between the forward wheels."[15]

His guides also foretold the invention of the typewriter in *Penetralia*: "I am almost moved to invent an automatic psychographe—that is, an artificial soul-writer. It may be constructed something like a piano, one brace or scale of keys to represent the elementary sounds; another and lower tier to represent a combination, and still another for a rapid recombination so that a person, instead of playing a piece of music, may touch off a sermon or a poem." Even the most skeptical scientist had to admit Andrew Jackson Davis was correct when he stated there were nine planets in the solar system—when science had only discovered seven: "In March, 1846 Andrew Jackson Davis said that there are nine planets in our solar system. At that time, astronomers knew only of seven (Mercury, Venus, Earth, Mars, Jupiter, Saturn, and Uranus). Neptune and Pluto were not discovered."[16]

THE STRATFORD POLTERGEIST

One day at dinner a package of six or eight silver spoons were all at once taken up and doubled up—bent double by no visible agency.
—*Reverend Austin Phelps*

Not every spirit is as evolved as Galen or Swedenborg. Some spirits can be very mischievous. *Poltergeist* is a German word for noisy ghost supposedly responsible for loud noises and levitating or throwing objects about. Sometimes these unruly spirits are even capable of slapping or tripping people, events which took place at the Phelps mansion in Stratford, Connecticut.

Back in 1639, when the town of Stratford was settled, a poltergeist was the last thing on the minds of Puritan settlers. Foremost in their minds was the desire to create a place where they could worship freely without the interference of a king or parliament. They chose the Native American village of Cupheag, located on Long Island Sound at the mouth of the Housatonic River. Their leader, Adam Blakeman, took a group of sixteen families to the town they named after Stratford-upon-Avon in England.

It grew from a small settlement into a large town. Originally, Trumbull and Bridgeport were sections of Stratford, as well as Shelton and Monroe. The 1820s brought change to Strafford's population when Connecticut abolished slavery. Many free blacks settled in the Stratford-Bridgeport area. Stratford remained largely rural until bridges were constructed in the 1840s and 1850s, which opened the Bridgeport area of Stratford to more development. The area's industrial growth attracted many immigrants from overseas, as well as residents from surrounding states.

The community continued to diversify as descendants of the founding Puritan families intermarried into other religions. Even Spiritualist practices once condemned by the Puritans were being tolerated. In 1848, many Stratford citizens, including Dr. Eliakim Phelps, were reading accounts of the Fox sisters and their Rochester rappings.

In 1849, Dr. Phelps purchased a three-story mansion at 1738 Elm Street from Captain George Dowell. The sea captain designed a hallway seventy feet long and twelve feet wide with twin staircases that matched the layout of his clipper ship. The fifty-nine-year-old Presbyterian clergyman hoped to retire in tranquility. He brought his young wife, three stepchildren—Anna, sixteen; Henry, eleven; and a six-year-old girl—and the couple's three-year-old son.

The Reverend Phelps was a man of his times. He was interested in mysticism, mesmerism and the Spiritualist movement in America—so much so that he decided to try a séance with a friend on March 4, 1850. However, they believed they were unable to contact any spirits. Apparently they were wrong. A few days later, on March 10, 1850, the family returned from church only to find their front door, which had been locked, wide open with a black mourning cloth over it. "Upon entering the dining room, they saw a female apparition laid out on the dinner table, as if on display for a wake. Then she vanished before their very eyes."[1]

Who was this intrusive female spirit? Some in Stratford believed it was the ghost of Goody Bassett. Rumor had it that the so-called witch was hanged on that very spot in 1651. She was the third witch to be hanged in New England. The first was Alis Young in Windsor, Connecticut, a town sixty miles north of Stratford.

It is no secret that the town's original settlers frowned on any form of paranormal activity. Reverend Blakeman, the pastor of Stratford's First Congregational Church, was fond of quoting the Holy Bible, which he brought from over England. It clearly stated, "Thou shalt not suffer a witch to live." In 1642, the general court took action against witches and made consulting with "a familiar spirit" a crime punishable by death.

Goody Bassett was quickly under suspicion when she and her family moved from the New Haven colony to nearby Stratford. Many of her neighbors complained of the abnormally cold weather and strange aches and pains that came over them in that very cold winter of 1650. Even illnesses seem to increase. Women, in particular, did not trust the newcomer. Several stepped forward to testify against Goody Bassett. They insisted that she had put curses on them, causing them physical torment and illnesses. Some of the women and young girls even claimed to witness Goody Bassett consorting with a mysterious being. Her trial attracted the attention of the governor of Connecticut, John Hayes. He presided over the trial, and magistrates Cullick and Clark sat on the bench with him. Stratford's deputies to the general court, Thomas Thornton and Philip Groves, were also there.[2] In what must have been a kangaroo court, the unfortunate woman was found guilty of the crime of witchcraft and hanged on Gallow's Brook in 1651.

If the spirit of Goody Bassett did visit the Phelps home, she created quite a ruckus. The minister and his family were startled by raps that were heard all over the house. They were very shocked to see objects move about the house while adults stood guard. In fact, "thirty stuffed clothing figures were created by unseen hands at inhuman speed and somehow teleported through the house while nobody was watching."[3] The family also found many pieces of silver bent by unseen hands. Even the children complained that they felt they were slapped by invisible hands.

In no way would Phelps have blamed the spirit of Goody Bassett. When he summoned the police, he was sure the intruder had been a robber. However, the police saw no evidence of a forced entry or valuables taken. Yet the home invasion was not an isolated incident. In the ensuing months, the poltergeist activity continued. Loud raps were heard all over the house, and objects moved around on their own. "Over the next six months, many odd things occurred, including (but not limited to), other effigies appearing; one of Phelps's sons being carried across a room by invisible hands; other family members being pinched and slapped by unseen forces; objects randomly moving through the air; furniture overturning of its own volition; windows breaking; food materializing from nowhere and pelting the family; and perhaps most notoriously, all manner of mysterious noises sounding at all hours—loud rappings, knockings and poundings as well as unexplained cries and shouts."[4]

Other strange events occurred. "On one occasion, Dr. Phelps was in his study alone, writing at his desk. He turned away for a moment and when he turned back he found that his sheet of paper, which had been blank, was now covered with strange-looking writing. An invisible presence had written 'very nice paper and ink for the devil.' The ink on the paper was still wet."[5]

Soon, accounts of the hauntings were published in the local newspaper. Dr. Phelps's son Austin was aghast at the unsavory publicity. A professor at Andover Theological Seminary, he was no believer in poltergeists. He was sure that there was a rational explanation. Perhaps sixteen-year-old Anna or eleven-year-old Henry was responsible for playing a childish trick?

Austin and a friend arranged to stay over two nights. They took turns guarding the doors. Even this vigilance had no effect on the spirits. They heard louds raps coming from the front door knocker; however, no one was in sight. How could that be? They also heard rappings upstairs coming from Anna's room. When they rushed in to catch the very nervous young lady in the act of knocking on the wall, "The young lady was in bed, covered up and out of reach of the door. We examined the panel and found dents where it had been struck."[6]

Other unexplainable incidents occurred at dinner. Spoons would fly out of pots on the table. Sometimes they were bent: "One day at dinner a package of six or eight silver spoons were all at once taken up and doubled up—bent double by no visible agency."[7] Later, the twisted spoons, which had been locked in a closet, were found perfectly straight with no signs of having ever been bent in two. According to Austin Phelps, there were dozens of such incidents.[8]

One spooky event, in particular, stood out. While his father was sitting alone in a small room at his desk, he heard incessant raps. Using an alphabet board, the spirit spelled out "put your hand under the table." When Reverend Phelps did as he was told, his hand "was grasped by a human hand, warm and soft."[9]

The minister's home was becoming a house of terror. The nighttime hours were the worst. They were filled with raps, strange voices, screams and other bizarre sounds, while the daylight hours saw objects sailing about through the rooms. Silverware bent and twisted, windows broke, papers scattered and tables and chairs danced across the floor as if they had come to life. And of course, the strange effigies continued to appear. It was reported in the *New Haven Journal* that "in a short space of time so many figures were constructed that it would not have been possible for a half a dozen women, working steadily for several hours, to have completed their design, and arrange the picturesque tableau. Yet these things happened in short space of time, with the whole house on the watch. In all, about 30 figures were constructed during this period."[10]

The Phelps family members were not the only witnesses to these bizarre event. In a letter to the *Boston Transcript*, Reverend Phelps said he could produce a "score of witnesses." Furthermore, these events occurred "more than a thousand times." He declared he had *seen things in motion more than a thousand times and in most cases when no visible power existed by which the motions could have been produced. I can produce scores of persons whose character for intelligence, piety, and competence to judge in the matter no one who know them will question, who*

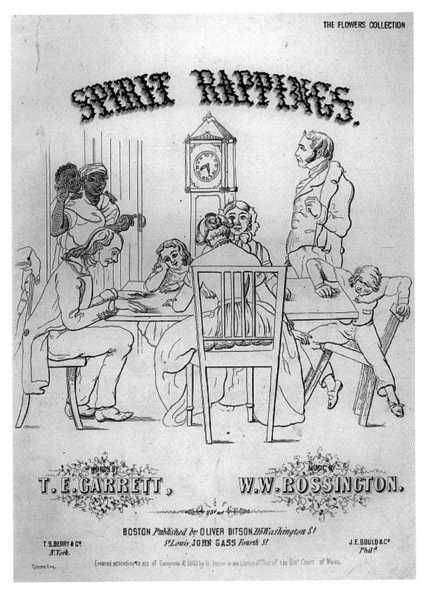

Spirit rapping was so popular, there was even sheet music, "Spirit Rappings." *Library of Congress.*

will make solemn oath that they have witnessed the same things. As for the reality of the facts they can be proven by a testimony a thousand-fold greater than ordinarily in our court of justice in cases of life and death.[11]

All this havoc took its toll on Reverend Phelps and his family. After seven months of psychic chaos, they decided to take the children back to Philadelphia. There, they spent a peaceful winter.

What caused the strange events at 1738 Elm Street? Could it be that Phelps, who had conducted a séance a few days before the disturbances began, opened a portal to the other side? Perhaps the family was being tormented by the angry spirit of Goody Bassett? Reverend Andrew Jackson Davis, who was called in to investigate, was not so sure. After his investigation of the Phelps residence, he asserted his belief in the genuineness of the activity. Davis asserted that the outbreaks were caused by "vital radiations" from Henry and Anna and that when the "magnetism" was at its strongest, objects were attracted to the two of them. However, he also believed that they could radiate a sort of "electricity" as well, which would propel objects away from them.[12]

Davis was correct in his assumption that Henry was involved in some manner. Several months later, long messages in intricate script appeared. This time, Henry admitted to writing the letters in a "mesmeric" state, which he interpreted for the benefit of his parents. The messages, he claimed, came from his deceased father. One spirit missive asked the boy to "obey dear Mr. Phelps in everything for he knows what is right and what is wrong."[13]

Spiritualists would point out that the confession only accounted for a few of the letters and did not explain the source of other communications, raps and poltergeist activity. The case created an enormous stir in the 1850s. Spiritualists throughout the United States cited the Stratford Poltergeist as proof of the New Dispensation sweeping the nation.[14]

THE MEDIUM WHO LEVITATED

*Suddenly, no one expected the group, Home rose into the air. I was holding his
hand and examined his feet were 30 cm above the ground.*
—Hartford Times, *August 1852*

During the heyday of Spiritualism, one medium stood head and
shoulders above all others—literally. Daniel Dunglas Home was seen
to fly eighty-five feet above the ground. To this day, scientists and magicians
cannot explain his remarkable feats of levitation. Even Houdini could
not duplicate his feat of levitating out a third-story window and returning
through another window in broad daylight. On December 13, 1868, Home's
friend Lord Lindsay heard him go into the next room and open the window.
In a few minutes, "Home appeared upright standing outside the window.
Daniel then opened the window and walked in, sat down and laughed."[1]

The most famous medium of the nineteenth century was born near
Edinburgh, Scotland, on March 20, 1833, the third child of seer Elizabeth
Home and William Home. It was rumored that Daniel's father was the
illegitimate son of Alexander, the Tenth Earl of Home. Unfortunately,
his father had to secure work as a millworker. The disgruntled man was
given to bouts of heavy drinking.[2] With little hope for improvement in their
impoverished circumstances, the couple felt it best to give their sickly infant
son to his aunt Mary Cook to raise.

Daniel exhibited uncanny phenomena early in life. His aunt swore that
she saw his cradle rocked on its own. As the boy began to talk, he mentioned

people only he could see. Mary, a pious woman, hardly knew what to make of it.

When her adopted son was nine, Mary and her husband immigrated to New London, Connecticut. Throughout his childhood, Daniel remained delicate, plagued by consumption. Instead of normal childhood pursuits, he spent solitary days walking in the woods or reading the Bible. His spirit friends became a source of comfort.

Occasionally, Home's earthly friend Edwin would accompany him on walks. The two thirteen-year-olds made a pact to make contact with each other if they should die.[3] It would seem like a morbid promise to modern sensibilities; however, early death was not uncommon in Victorian times. In any event, Daniel put the matter out of his mind when he and his family moved to Troy, New York. A few years later, though, he was awakened in the middle of the night by a bright light at the foot of his bed, which he "knew" was Edwin's spirit. Three days later, a letter arrived stating that Edwin had died of malignant dysentery.

While most young men would be startled by a visit from a deceased friend, Daniel believed his clairvoyance was a gift from God. He remained calm, a few days later, when he heard three loud raps during the night. According to Home, the raps sounded as if the headboard had been stuck by a hammer.

The seventeen-year-old promptly told Aunt Mary. At first she did not believe him. Then, she, too, started to hear the loud raps coming from the breakfast table. She threw a chair at him and said, "You have brought the devil to our household!" A devout Christian, she sent the sensitive lad to a Congregational minister, who could not find anything wrong him. Next, she sought help from a Methodist minister, who agreed that the raps were the work of the devil but could offer no solution to the problem. Finally, Daniel was sent to the local Baptist minister, who prayed over the lad. Every time the minister uttered the name of a holy person, the gentle raps became more passionate.[4]

The best advice the clergymen could offer was to ignore the phenomenon. That did not sit well with Mary, who decided to take the matter into her own hands. When she saw a table move by itself, she placed a Bible on top and tried to keep it still—to no avail.[5] It was as if some unseen force had control of the table. Torn between her devotion to God and her love for her nephew, she chose God. Aunt Mary promptly asked Daniel to leave her home.

The teenager soon found lodging in various households in Willimantic and Lebanon, Connecticut. In March 1851, the slim auburn-haired medium conducted his first public séance. Hartford newspaper reporter W.R. Hayden witnessed the table moving "in any direction we asked it to" without any human hands touching it.[6]

The gentleman medium did not charge for his séances, although he would accept lodging and gifts on occasion. Unlike most mediums, who produce phenomena in darkened rooms, D.D. Home's séances were held in brightly lit areas. He was determined to show the public that there were no tricks up his sleeve. Even in daylight, ghostly hands appeared to move tables, play music and even move lettered cards to spell out messages from the dead.

In August 1852, Home's mediumship took a new development when he visited the South Manchester home of Ward Cheney, a successful silk manufacturer. The slender youth was observed rising up to the ceiling by a reporter from the *Hartford Times*: "Suddenly, no one expected the group, Home rose into the air. I was holding his hand and examined his feet were 30 cm above the ground. All Home's body throbbed, a confusion of emotions ranging from joy to fear, choking his words. Again and again he levitated. In the third, climbed to the roof of the apartment, where touched hands and feet."[7]

In 1852, while Home was staying with Rufus Elmer in Springfield, Massachusetts, Harvard professor David Wells and the poet and editor of the *New York Evening Post*, William Cullen Bryant, attended his séances. They were allowed to inspect the séance room, and the séances were held in a "well-lit" area. The two agreed: "We know that we were not imposed upon nor deceived." It was also reported that at one of Home's demonstrations, five men of heavy build (850 pounds together) sat on a table, but it still moved, and others saw "a tremulous phosphorescent light gleam over the walls."[8]

Home continued to refuse payment for his séances. Eventually, he planned to make his living by becoming a doctor. However, he became ill with tuberculosis in early 1854, putting an end to his medical studies. On the advice of his physicians, Home decided to recuperate in Europe. He gave his last American séance in Hartford, Connecticut, on March 14, 1855. According to Frank L. Burr, editor of the *Hartford Times*, the tablecloth was lifted, and a guitar some five or six feet from the medium played on its own. The music from spirit was unique: "Portions of it were filled with a certain soft and wild melody that seemed to be an echo of other music far away, and for the exquisite sweetness of which there are no words."[9]

When Home arrived in Europe, he changed his name to Daniel Dunglas Home. The charming medium soon met a believer in Spiritualism, William Cox, who had the medium as a guest in his large London hotel at 53, 54 and 55 Jermyn Street. Cox was so enthralled by Home's abilities that he introduced the young man to many of his society friends. Early on, Home was giving séances for scientist Sir David Brewster and novelists Sir Edward Bulwer-Lytton and Thomas Adolphus Trollope. It was not long before Daniel Dunglas Home hosted séances attended by Elizabeth Barrett Browning, Napoleon III, the Empress Eugenie and even Leo Tolstoy. Sir William Crookes (1832–1919) and Dr. Robert Hare (1781–1858) stated that, in their opinion, the phenomena manifested by Home were genuine.

Home amazed British citizens with his phenomenal séances. In a letter dated October 23, 1855, Thomas Dalling Barlee gave this account of a séance, which was published in the *Yorkshire Spiritual Telegraph*:

> *Mr. Hume then said, "As the spirits seem inclined to give us some music, let us hear that first, and in the meantime, if the paper and pencil are put under the cloth, I have no doubt little Watty will have written something before the music is finished." Mr. Rymer then placed the pencil and paper under the tablecloth, and the accordion soon, without any visible handling, played "Home, Sweet Home." [Here follows a description of the music.] After the accordion ceased, Mr. Rymer said, "Now let us see whether little Watty has written anything for papa," when instantly five raps came calling for the alphabet, and then there was spelt, "Dear papa, I have done my very best," and on Mr. Rymer's taking up the paper he found written on it, "Dear papa, dear mama, Watt," and on comparing the handwriting with that contained in one of his last letters before he died, it was found to be exactly resembling the writing there, particularly the capital letters.*[10]

From all accounts, Daniel Dunglas Home cut a dashing, though pale, figure. The tall young man with blue eyes and auburn hair was particularly fastidious in his attire. Even though his education was limited, he had had the ability to converse on a variety of subjects and could play the piano. Home was a welcome guest in the drawing room as well as a phenomenal medium in the séance room. He gave séances for well-connected clients throughout Europe. Some early guests at Home's sittings included the scientist Sir David Brewster, novelist Sir Edward Bulwer-Lytton and poetess Elizabeth Barrett Browning. She was convinced that the medium was genuine; however, her husband, Robert Browning, remained a skeptic.

As Home traveled across Europe, he gave séances for Napoleon III and Queen Sophia of the Netherlands. She wrote, "I saw him four times . . . I felt a hand tipping my finger; I saw a heavy golden bell moving alone from one person to another; I saw my handkerchief move alone and return to me with a knot . . . He himself is a pale, sickly, rather handsome young man but without a look or anything which would either fascinate or frighten you. It is wonderful. I am so glad I have seen it."[11]

Daniel Dunglas Home had an uncanny knack for attracting loyal followers. One of his admirers was a wealthy widow, Jane Lyon. She was so besotted by the medium's spiritual abilities that she adopted the thirty-three-year-old Home. She even insisted on taking care of her new "son" with a generous gift of sum of £60,000. Apparently, Mrs. Lyon had a change of heart and sued Home for the return of the money. When Home lost the case, he had to refund his "mother" the full amount. It is interesting to note that Home remained as popular as ever after the unsavory publicity.

In his travels, he continued to perform levitations and materialize objects. "In his presence very heavy Victorian furniture rocked and floated in the air, in other séances hands materialized and traveled round the Circle of sitters, on other occasions an accordion wafted along playing of its own accord without anyone touching it."[12]

He amazed people by doing this in broad daylight. He also would take red-hot burning coals and hold them in his hands without being burned. Sometimes, with the permission of his spirit guides, he would hand them to others in the séance to hold. Their hands also remained unscarred. He was never caught in fraud, even though many in the Christian communities tried to categorize him as a fake.[13]

While living in Europe, Home married twice. In 1858, he married Alexandria de Kroll, the seventeen-year-old daughter of a Russian aristocrat. The marriage, which lasted four years, produced a son, Gregoire. Home was devastated when Alexandria, ill with tuberculosis, died in 1862. Later, in October 1871, the medium married Julie de Gloumeline, another wealthy Russian woman, whom he met in St. Petersburg. At the age of thirty-eight, Home retired to the Mediterranean due to poor health. He passed to spirit on June 21, 1886, and was buried in France.[14]

According to his widow, one of D.D. Home's finest qualities was his charity. As with true generosity, it was done in secret without publicity. After his death, his widow found many incidences of kindness without thought of himself revealed in her husband's correspondence. "Now it is an unknown artist for whose brush Home's generous efforts had found employment, now a distressed worker writes of his sick wife's life saved by comforts Home provided, now a mother thanks him for a start in life for her son. How much time and thought he devoted to helping others when the circumstances of his own life would have led most men to think only of their own needs and cares."[15] Sir Arthur Conan Doyle revealed that Home was also known to roam the battlefields in France with cigars in his pocket to hand out to the wounded. One German officer wrote a letter Home to thank him for saving his life when Home carried the wounded man. Another man wrote, "Shall I ever prove worth of all the good you have done me?"[16]

Daniel Dunglas Home. *Photograph by Felix Nadar, Wikimedia Commons.*

The question remains, though, was Daniel Douglas Home a charming charlatan or a gifted medium who conducted more than fifteen hundred séances? Many, such as Sir Arthur Conan Doyle, an ardent Spiritualist, believed in him. According to Doyle, D.D. Home excelled as a trance medium, clairvoyant and physical phenomena. How then were his

Daniel Dunglas Home levitating at the home of Ward Cheney on August 8, 1852.
Les Mystères de la Science by Louis Figuier.

levitations accomplished? Home claimed not to know himself. He stated that an "unseen power" simply came over him and lifted him into the air.

While a Spiritualist such as Doyle might find this a plausible explanation, others believed that Home was a charlatan. One researcher, Frank Podmore, was convinced that Home was a fraud whose feats such as handling hot coals could be performed by sleight of hand. Another skeptic, Robert Browning, claimed that the "spirit-hand" observed in the séance room was a false hand attached on the end of Home's arm. Magician Harry Houdini even boasted that "he could duplicate Home's feat of levitating in and out of the third-floor windows at Lord Adare's home, but he canceled the event without explanation."[17]

To his credit, D.D. Home allowed himself to be tested by Sir William Crookes (1832–1919). Between 1870 and 1873, the physicist conducted experiments on three mediums: Florence Cook, Kate Fox and Home. His final report, *Researches into the Phenomena of Spiritualism*, published in 1874, concluded that D.D. Home did, in fact, produce genuine phenomena. Dr. Crookes went so far as to design a special cage, one with an opening large enough for just one hand. When Crookes placed an accordion inside, the medium was able to play tunes such as "Home Sweet Home" on the instrument. Even more evidential, the accordion continued to play after Home let go of his thumb and middle finger with no person touching it:

> *After a materialization was heard to join the Circle and touched Mrs. Crookes, the accordion was played and Crookes recorded that, "we had a beautiful accompaniment, the chirping and singing of the birds being heard along with the accordion." Raps were heard and a luminous cloud appeared: "Immediately the white luminous cloud was seen to travel . . . to Mrs. Wm. C.'s hand, and a small sprig of the plant was put into it. She had her hand then patted by a delicate female hand . . . The table was now heard to be moving, and it was seen to glide slowly."*

Sir William Crookes concluded that Home had proven "beyond doubt" the existence of a "psychic force."[18]

6
REMARKABLE
SPIRITUALIST HEALINGS

Sorrow, grief, fear, or any extraordinary emotion, will cause disease; so to be well,
be cheerful, and wear a pleasant countenance.[1]
— *Dr. James Rogers Newton*

There are many aspects to Spiritualism in Connecticut. While Daniel Dunglas Home was best known for physical mediumship, Reverend Andrew Jackson Davis was famous as a trance medium as well as a remarkable healer. Healing is another important aspect of Spiritualism. In a time when the average person was lucky to live to fifty, the laying on of hands healing and magnetic healers were in demand during the second half of the 1800s.

In addition to Davis, there were other Spiritualist healers who restored Connecticut citizens to health. For example, Mark Twain's wife, Olivia, was cured by Spiritualist healer Dr. James Rogers Newton. She had a tragic accident as a teenager when she fell on ice and suffered paralysis. Her desperate father paid faith healer James Rogers Newton $1,500 to cure his daughter. This was the fee Dr. Newton charged those worth over $1,000—for those with less income, healing sessions were free. The faith healer prayed over Olivia for a few moments, and then she took several steps. "According to Twain, Newton pulled back the shades, letting light into the room for the first time in two years, and said, 'Now we will sit up, my child.' Miraculously, with a prayer, Dr. Newton aided Livy in walking a few steps."[2]

Spiritualist healer Dr. James Rogers Newton was born in September 1810 in Newport, Rhode Island. He was a direct descendant of John Rogers, who was burned at the stake. Even though Newton knew that he had healing powers early in life, he chose to wait until later in life to utilize them. After twenty years as a successful merchant, he was ready to devote his life to healing others. He particularly wished to demonstrate how the vital magnetic energy of a healer could produce an instantaneous cure: "In 1853, Dr. Newton was a passenger on the steamer, *Golden Gate*, from Panama to San Francisco. The second day yellow fever broke out among the 1,300 passengers which also included several physicians. The fever raged for eight days, with seventy-four persons dying and their bodies being consigned to the ocean. The ship's surgeon lost every patient but one that he attended. Dr. Newton lost none."[3]

Soon, Dr. Newton was doing healings in Cincinnati, Baltimore, New York and Boston. New Haven resident Henry Hooker traveled to Boston for a session with Dr. Newton; the wealthy carriage dealer had a throat problem that reduced his voice to a whisper. After a brief fifteen minutes of manipulations, the doctor assured his patient "his voice would be as strong as ever. He not only regained his voice but graciously praised the healer."[4]

The famous nineteenth-century healer performed miracle healings in New Haven and Hartford as well. He primarily did laying-on-of-hands healing. At the height of his career, he was seeing one hundred patients a day. Thousands gave sworn testimonies to his gift of healing in his book *The Modern Bethesda or The Gift of Healing Restored*,[5] written in 1879. Even so, the doctor remained a humble man, according to his personal secretary, Austin A. Hill: "From his lips I never heard a profane or obscene word or expression, and nothing seemed to offend him. He was a man of powerful physique and strong passions, and when he heard the word humbug used and applied to him, the fire of those dark hazel eyes and a simple admonition were sufficient to make the stoutest and most hardened, quail and humbly apologize, or quickly leave his presence."[6]

One of the Connecticut citizens to praise Dr. Newton was Hartford carriage dealer Henry Hooker, who regained his voice after only one treatment. The doctor used no drugs and performed no surgery—just fifteen minutes of magnetic healing. Hooker gave this testimony, which was published in the *New Haven Courier* in June 1863:

A Marvelous Cure

Mr. H. Hooker, well known as an extensive carriage dealer in this city, for six years past has been troubled with a difficulty of the throat which seriously interfered with articulation—reducing his voice to a mere whisper. During all this time he has not spoken one loud word—a truth that hundreds of his acquaintances among our business men can vouch for— and, of course, a man so situated would resort to every means that seemed to promise a glimmer of hope of removing the affliction. Until a short time ago, however, he did not succeed in meeting with any relief. Being in Boston a little while since, he was persuaded, having almost ceased to look for recovery, to consult Dr. J.R. Newton, a physician of that city; and Dr. N., to the surprise and delight of Mr. Hooker, after going through with a very brief series of manipulations—fifteen minutes was all the time consumed, if we properly understood our informant—assured his patient that his voice was as strong as ever! Strange as it may appear, the friends of Mr. Hooker in this city have had oral evidence of the truthfulness of the cure from Mr. Hooker's own lips! He has quite regained his voice, and very naturally uses it a good deal in praise of the physician who effected the restoration.[7]

Soon after, the following correspondence took place:

New Haven, Conn., June 9th, 1863.
Dr. J.R. Newton, Boston, Mass.

Dear Sir: The undersigned, having witnessed the remarkable results of your treatment of several of our citizens, would cordially invite you to visit our city, and further extend the beneficial effects of your powers.

Very respectfully yours,

Henry Hooker, Edwin Marble,
Isaac Thompson, Philo Chatfield,
E. Benjamin, Jas. F. Babcock,
J. Collins, Geo. Brown,
W. A. Ensign, Smith Merwin,
N. Willcox, Arthur D. Osborne,
R. Chapman, Gardner Morse,
Wm. B. Johnson, James Brewster.[8]

Dr. Newton accepted the invitation from Henry Hooker and his fellow citizens. He invited all who were not well to come—even those without the means to pay. His visits to New Haven and Hartford were very well received. He made a most favorable impression on Austin A. Hill, who first met the doctor in New Haven during the summer of 1863. Huge crowds attended his healing session held on New York Street in New Haven.

The doctor was as efficient as he was compassionate. When a patient arrived, he or she was given a ticket with a number on it. Each was admitted in an orderly manner. Dr. Newton treated everyone, regardless of his or her means to pay him. He placed a card over the door of one of the parlors on which was written "Persons who cannot afford to pay are cordially invited to come without money and without price."[9] Some were cured in one session. Others with deafness, epilepsy, consumption, tumors or damaged spines required additional treatments. "Those diseases that are most certain of being cured by one operation are weak spines and all kinds of female diseases, internal ulcers, loss of voice, diseased liver, kidneys and heart, weakness of limbs, dyspepsia, rheumatism, bronchitis, diabetes and nervous debility."[10]

Several cases stood out in Arthur Hill's recollection. The first, Miss Caroline F. Davis, of Guilford, Connecticut, was brought on a bed sixteen miles. Afflicted with spinal disease, she had not walked for six years or spoken above a whisper for four years—she was cured instantly. She walked away rejoicing and talked as freely as anyone. Miss Davis later visited the doctor in New York. She said she came to thank him for what he did for her three years earlier. Mrs. William Toohy of Hartford was so weak that she had to be carried into the room in her husband's arms. She had a spinal injury and was instantly cured, able to walk out of his office. Reverend D. Carroll was present for several healings as well. He witnessed Dr. Newton instantaneously remove a tumor from Comfort S. Farrer of Fair Haven. He could hardly believe her eyes, as the woman had suffered from a large tumor that was seven inches long and four inches wide for many months.[11]

Reporters from the *Hartford Courant*, the *New Haven Times* and the *New Haven Register* all carried stories of Dr. Newton's miraculous healings. In July 1863, the *New Haven Courier* added several names to the list of those healed in Connecticut: Albert Hyde of Orange, Connecticut, cured of an ulcer on the leg. Sarah Recor, who was speechless for nine months, spoke again, as did Mrs. Robert Bassette of Derby, Connecticut, who had not spoken for four years. Miss Martha Hotchkiss added her praise. The twenty-one-year-old woman from Westville had been so sick that she was unable to get out of bed for two years. After her session with Dr. Newton, she now was able to get up each day and could take care of herself. Another patient, ten-year-old Jessie Mallory, was cured of hip disease, and an older woman, Harriet Parker, who lived on Canal Street in New Haven, was relieved of her rheumatism. Finally, Miss Kate White, lame for three years, was instantly cured.[12]

When a reporter from the *New Haven Times* visited, he observed, "There were more than fifty people waiting for treatment on hot August day in 1863—the majority were treated for free." One reporter decided to return to the York Street apartment in New Haven that served as a clinic for Dr. Newton. He was amazed by the sight of "people of all ages and ailments—about fifty patiently awaiting their turn to see Newton." They included "the paralytic, the rheumatic, the lame, the halt, sufferers from curved and weak spines (there were a number of these, chiefly females) pale victims, of chronic internal maladies, those pain-worn features told of weary years of hopeless suffering, rugged men with hands or limbs distorted by rheumatism or accidental injuries. Sufferers from disorder longs, stomach, liver, eye, every thing seemingly sat waiting their turn to be healed."[13]

Dr. Newton had some very original ideas about healing. Besides his belief that spirit magnetism may be used for healing, he occasionally recommended other remedies along with magnetic treatments such as the persistent use of hot water, that is, pouring hot water on the back of the head for thirty minutes three times a week in cases of insanity. By the way, Andrew Jackson Davis also recommend pouring hot water over the head to rid the insane of possession by depraved spirits. Newton also favored the use of hot water treatment for asthma.

He also believed that wearing garters made feet cold and crippled limbs. He also warned his patients "to never sleep or sit with hand up to the head; it will cause heart disease, consumption, liver complaints, and dyspepsia." Finally, he believed that spirit magnetism—the life principle—may be imparted from one to another and is the only power to heal the sick.[14] Often he was asked the secret of his success. The kindly good doctor would reply, "The healer must be imbued with the love principle."[15]

While some of the patients were not restored by the doctor's magnetic powers, others were completely healed by his magnetism. "Newton loved to touch a patient and say 'All well. Now you are a new man. Run I say.' Miraculously, the lame did just that—even paralyzed patients."[16] For example, the *New Haven Resister* listed Mr. Merwin W. Davis of New Boston, Connecticut, among those cured of paralysis. "He came in on Thursday, swinging along on crutches—the lower part of body and both legs paralyzed for three years." According to the reporter, the paralyzed man "walk[ed] dance[ed] and then sat down and cried like a child in his too great joy"[17] Miss MaryAnn Dunham of South Windsor, Connecticut, who had been lame for ten years, also was able to walk again after spending a few minutes with Dr. Newton. Another invalid, Miss Hannah Whittlesey, was so weak that she was laid on a sofa. The Wethersfield resident had been bedridden for seventeen years, yet ten minutes later she walked out of Newton's office. Afterward, she was able to return to taking care of herself and her home.[18]

She was not alone. Many others received healings from Dr. Newton. Here is a list of people who reported they had been cured by the doctor in his Hartford office, many of whom received treatment and afterward called and reported themselves completely cured:

> *Mrs. Russell Landfair, Fair Haven, Conn., ill for five years, walked out of the office, a well woman.*
>
> *Mrs. Charlotte Savoy's son Lewis, 84 George Street, New Haven, epileptic fits five years, cured.*
>
> *Mrs. Sarah Ford, Ridgefield, Conn., spine and female problems, cured.*
>
> *Mrs. Mary Anne Dunham, East Windsor, Conn., very lame, could not walk.*
>
> *Mrs. Wm. Luthrop, Lebanon, Conn., spinal weakness, cured.*
>
> *William Keith, postmaster, Tolland, Conn., spasms, cure.*
>
> *Mrs. Frances A. Canfield, Seymour, Conn., spine disease, able to walk one treatment.*
>
> *Miss Mary E. Scott, Danbury, Conn., lame nine years, walk without her crutches.*
>
> *Miss Celia Merwin, Higganum, Conn., very lame, but cured instantly.*
>
> *Mrs. P.B. Hinsdale, 171 Temple Street. New Haven, weak eyes cured in five minutes.*
>
> *W.C. Waters, 129 Crown Street, New Haven, weak eyes cured in fifteen minutes. She no longer needed glasses to read.*
>
> *Mrs. Harriet Parker, 106 Canal street, New Haven, rheumatism since childhood, completely cured.*
>
> *Miss Elizabeth Keith, Union, Conn., vocal organs paralyzed, instantly cured and able to speak.*
>
> *Mrs. Jane Anne Hough, Hartford, heart disease cured.*
>
> *Mrs. Ellen Wentworth, 7 Sheldon street, Hartford, consumption cured.*
>
> *Mrs. Darius R. Stockwell, Putnam, Conn., blind four years and three months, able to read fine print without glasses.*
>
> *Mrs. Harris Smith, High street, New Haven, Conn., cancer completely cured.*

Geo. Brown's son, jeweler. Chapel Street, New Haven, weak spine made it unable to walk, instantly able to walk well.

Wm. Barber, Westville, Conn., cured of paralysis.

Mr. Francis L. Cady, West Stafford, Conn., dyspepsia for ten years was cured.

Mrs. Francis L. Cady, West Stafford, Conn., lame, was able to walk.

Daughter of Mr. Francis L. Cady, West Stafford, Conn., one eye was totally blind, the other nearly blind. Her sight was restored to sight to read fine print.

Henry B. Cook, Bristol, Conn., speechless seven months, instantly able to speak.

Mr. George A. Mack, Windsor, Conn., his lame knee and tumor, cured in five minutes.

Jabez West, Tolland, Conn, his asthma of thirty years cured with one treatment.[19]

Many, such as Mrs. F.L. Wright of Bristol, Connecticut, an invalid for six years, were extremely grateful. She wrote in a letter dated November 21, 1863, that after her twenty-minute session with Dr. Newton on October 1863, she felt like one "risen from the dead."

A LETTER TO DR. NEWTON

Bristol Conn., Nov. 21, 1863

My Dear Sir—

May God bless you! It is now three weeks since I was healed. It is eighteen years since I became a confirmed invalid and six years since I could walk ill I saw you. My friends are astonished to see me so well . . . sister Eddy, who was bed-fast. She continues well. Some say this the work of the devil. If so, they had better change their doxology. I have received a great blessing. I almost feel like one risen from the dead.

Your Grateful friend,
Mrs. L.F. Wright.[20]

Dr. Newton was not without his critics. Some believed his laying-on-of-hands healing was the work of the devil. For instance, one church disapproved of parishioner Perry Peckham seeing a Spiritualist healer—even though the

Gilead man had been wracked with rheumatism for seven years. He could barely hobble on crunches into the treatment room. He had to have his wife's assistance. A large crowd followed the couple into the room. Within ten minutes, his limbs were as supple as ever. Perry happily walked out, to the intense excitement of all present. It was an emotional scene, with tears of joy streaming down the faces of the onlookers.[21]

Mark Twain with his wife, Olivia. *Mark Twain House and Museum, Hartford, Connecticut.*

After such an amazing healing, the residents of Gilead could talk of nothing else. Once the church officials heard about Peckham's restoration to health, they called a special meeting to discuss the turn of events. When they read their charge of conspiring with the devil, Mrs. Peckham stood up to speak. She said, "If anyone of your family a cripple for seven years, and had seem him suffer constant pain, and had him to wait upon as I have done, you would not mind if it was the Devil that cured him!"[22]

7

HARRIET BEECHER STOWE

A Spiritual Life

I did not write it. God wrote it. I merely did his dictation.
—Harriet Beecher Stowe

Noted residents of Connecticut were becoming increasingly interested in the psychic forces, including members of the Beecher family: Harriet, Charles and Isabella. During the late nineteenth century, the Beechers were one of the most influential families in Connecticut. The family patriarch, Lyman Beecher, was a fiery Congregational preacher. He married twice, fathering thirteen children. His most famous offspring, Harriet Elisabeth Beecher, was born on June 14, 1811, in Litchfield, Connecticut. Her mother was Roxana Foote. Her brother was noted social reformer Henry Ward Beecher, and her half-sister, Isabella Beecher Hooker, was a well-known suffragette and Spiritualist.

Harriet's father believed in educating women, and he encouraged his daughter Catharine to open a school for women. One of Catharine's first pupils, Harriet developed a deep love of literature and later enjoyed discussing books with her friends at the Semi-Colon Club, where she met widower Calvin Ellis Stowe. They were married on January 6, 1836, and the couple had seven children together, including twin daughters.

Harriet's new husband favored the abolition of slavery. The Stowes supported the Underground Railroad, a network of secret routes and safe houses that helped runaway slaves escape to Canada. When Congress passed the Fugitive Slave Law in 1850, Harriet Beecher Stowe was inspired to write *Uncle Tom's Cabin*; "I did not write it. God wrote it. I merely did his dictation."[1]

She wanted to "write something that would make this whole nation feel what an accursed thing slavery is."[2] Through her iconic characters of Tom, Eva and Topsy, she made Northerners aware of the impact of slavery on the family, particularly children. The book was first printed in installments, and the first one appeared on June 5, 1851. The installments were reorganized and sold as a book that soon became a best-seller, translated into sixty languages. When Harriet visited the White House, Abraham Lincoln greeted her with these words: "So you are the little lady who wrote the book that started this Great War."[3]

Writing was a necessity for Harriet Beecher Stowe. Throughout her marriage to a sickly husband, Harriet was compelled to bolster their budget with earnings from writing. She was keenly aware of a married woman's financial position. Harriet also campaigned for the married women's rights, arguing in 1869 that "the position of a married woman is, in many respects, precisely similar to that of the Negro slave. She can make no contract and hold no property; whatever she inherits or earns becomes at that moment the property of her husband. . . . Though he acquired a fortune through her, or though she earned a fortune through her talents, he is the sole master of it, and she cannot draw a penny."[4]

While most people know Harriet Beecher Stowe as a literary figure and reformer, few realize that she was interested in Spiritualism. She was not alone in her belief. Captain Stowe also embraced Spiritualism as a child and saw ghosts; as an adult, he claimed to regularly see the spirit of his first wife. Other prominent people shared the couple's belief in Spiritualism. They included *New York Tribune* editor Horace Greeley and Susan B. Anthony, who like many feminists was drawn to the faith because it accepted women as mediums and leaders.

Harriet's interested in Spiritualism may have been due to her brother Reverend Henry Beecher. When he hypnotized in her 1843, he led her to believe that she had visited a spiritual land during the session. She adored her minister brother and stood by him even when accused of adultery, his name attached to a national scandal. Her husband, Calvin, was also interested in the spirits. He often saw ghosts and fairies as a child. The couple spoke openly about their son Samuel, who died in the cholera epidemic in 1849. Their interest in Spiritualism increased with the death of their son Henry in 1857. When her nineteen-year-old son drowned in the Connecticut River, his mother feared that her boy may not have made his peace with God.

Victorians had many superstitions about death: curtains were drawn and clocks stopped at the time of death. Mirrors were immediately covered because the living believed that the dead become trapped in the glass's reflection. Mourning had stringent rules as well. Widows and widowers were expected to dress in black for two years and the parents of a child for nine months.[5]

Harriet coped with her grief by working in her garden. However, she felt Henry's presence everywhere, particularly in the house, where she had his pictures and presents she had planned to give him. This fixation on his death became too intense for her. She decided to go to Italy in the summer of 1859 and stayed with American friends in Florence. There she met a powerful medium, Mrs. E, who helped her to feel close to "my Henry and other departed friends."[6] Harriet told her husband, Calvin, about spirit writing, in which script appears on paper without hands or pen or pencil, and communicating with "various historical people."[7]

Calvin had his own tales to share. He had heard a guitar strum, yet no person was physically present. Harriet believed it was Calvin's first wife, Eliza. Far from being jealous of Calvin communicating with his first wife, Harriet encouraged him. She advised her husband to place the guitar in his bedroom so he could hear from her again.[8]

Harriet enjoyed her own time with the spirit world. When she visited mediums, she was careful in her questions to the departed. When she spoke to the spirit of Charlotte Brontë, using a Ouija board, she asked for evidence. The medium, who did not know the spirit purported to be the author of *Jane Eyre*, tranced these words in reply to questions of Harriet Beecher Stowe:

When were you born?
April 1816

When did you die?
March 1855

Do you retain the same traits of character that distinguished you here?
Not altogether. My principle characteristic was constitutional absence of hope. Now I am at Peace. Inasmuch as there is no call for hope where I am.[9]

When she asked Brontë's spirit "What constitutes happiness?" the planchette spelled out this message: "Each one of us has some peculiar mission. We are happy in that, and we have what to you is an unknown

Harriet Beecher Stowe. *Harriet Beecher Stowe Center, Hartford, Connecticut.*

Right: Reverend Calvin Stowe. *Harriet Beecher Stowe Center, Hartford, Connecticut.*

Below: Home of Harriet Beecher Stowe. *Harriet Beecher Stowe Center, Hartford, Connecticut.*

feeling of perfect peace."[10] Finally, Harriet asked this of the spirit of Charlotte Brontë: "What must we do to prepare for peace in that world [the other side]?" The spirit answered, "Read God's word and grieve not."[11] Harriet was delighted by the message.

Not all of her friends, however, shared her enthusiasm for spirit communication. When Harriet wrote author George Eliot, "I cannot get over the impression that I have had a conversation with Charlotte Brontë," Eliot was skeptical. [12] She called the séance a "degrading folly."[13] Nevertheless, Harriet remained firm in her belief. She even brought a planchette back to Hartford so she could conduct her own séances for Calvin and the twins.[14]

The Stowes also visited Kate Fox at the home of Dr. Taylor. The famous physical medium did not disappoint the group. They witnessed phosphorous light, a floating rose and a materialized pencil that wrote a message. As one sitter later recalled, "A guitar was raised up over our heads and played on. My husband who is a very stout man weighing two hundred pounds was moved back from the table five feet to the wall chair and all, and then again placed at the table."[15] While Harriet marveled at Kate Fox's mediumship, she began to have doubts about Fox's integrity. When it came to the spiritual, Harriet had every confidence in the invisible intelligent spirits—more so than the medium.[16]

Even so, Harriet Beecher Stowe continue to visit mediums. As late as 1883, she wrote her sister Isabella to tell her she had found comfort in a session with a medium who made contact with Harriet's lost son Fred. Later, when Isabella received a message from her deceased nephew, Harriet asked for a copy of it. In a letter to Oliver Wendell Holmes in 1876, Harriet said that she believed that the phenomena of Spiritualism would one day be proven by science. She further stated that she "had no faith in mediums who practice for money."[17]

Following the death of her husband in 1886, Harriet declined in health. Her neighbor Mark Twain recalled her last years in his autobiography: "Her mind had decayed, and she was a pathetic figure. She wandered about all the day long in the care of a muscular Irish woman . . . Sometimes we would hear gentle music in the drawing-room and would find her there at the piano singing ancient and melancholy songs with infinitely touching effect."[18]

In a bittersweet end to a long and spiritual life, Harriet Beecher Stowe joined her beloved husband, Calvin, on July 1, 1896, at age eighty-five in Hartford, Connecticut. Her three surviving children placed a rose-colored obelisk on her grave. The inscription chiseled on the granite monument read, "Her children rise up and call her blessed."

8

THE WHITE HOUSE MEDIUM

My child, you possess a very singular gift; but that it is of God, I have no doubt.
—Abraham Lincoln

Harriet Beecher Stowe was so famous in her day that even President Lincoln took note of her book *Uncle Tom's Cabin*. Yet there is no mentioned in the history books of Nettie Colburn Maynard. Her White House séances were kept hush-hush. Even today, few historians acknowledge the Hartford medium who conducted séances for Mary Todd Lincoln and the president after the death of their son Willie in February 1862. The nation grieved along with Willie's parents. Confederate president Jefferson Davis also gave his condolences.

While Lincoln kept his grief private, as he focused on work, his wife was anxious to contact Willie. One medium quickly caught her attention, Nettie Colburn from Hartford, Connecticut. Mrs. Cranston Laurie introduced Mrs. Lincoln to the petite medium in early 1863. Both Mr. and Mrs. Laurie, as well as their daughter Belle Miller, were known to be "under the spiritual influence." All three were mediums, and Belle excelled as a physical medium.

During Nettie Colburn's first séance for Mrs. Lincoln, a deceased family physician, Dr. Bamford, spoke through her for over an hour. The trance medium awoke to hear Mrs. Lincoln exclaim, "This young lady must not leave Washington. I feel she must stay here, and Mr. Lincoln must hear what we have heard. It is all-important, and he must hear it."[1] The First Lady even arranged a job for Nettie at the Agriculture Department to ensure the medium's close proximity.

Who was this extraordinary medium who had captured Mrs. Lincoln's attention? None other than Nettie Colburn, who was born in Connecticut in 1841. As child, she lived with her parents in Coventry and often visited her father's family in nearby Bolton, Connecticut. Life was tranquil in the country, until one evening in the winter of 1845. The family was sitting around an old-fashioned wooden table when they started to hear noises. Not unlike the Phelps family, the Colburns heard a series of raps. Then, the wooden table began to move, and loud sounds were heard by everyone in the room. "Before anyone had spoken the sound was repeated with equal force, and seemed to jar the entire room."[2] Nettie's mother was frightened, especially when she could not explain the outside source for the loud raps.

Her father, who was absent at the time, was apparently intrigued by spirit phenomena. In fact, he was fascinated by table tipping, which was becoming popular. In 1855, he invited a young man, Thomas Cook, to demonstrate table tipping in their Hartford residence. Soon Nettie was engaged in table tipping as well.

By 1856, the young medium was doing automatic writing. Her father, who wanted to be sure his daughter was receiving messages from spirits, decided to test the spirit. He asked the spirit who would win the upcoming election: John C. Frémont or James Buchanan. Nettie took a pencil in her right hand and wrote a response from the spirit, "Buchanan." When James Buchanan won the election the next day, her father was amazed, as he fully expected John C. Frémont to win.[3]

Later, on December 24, 1856, the fifteen-year-old medium held her first demonstration of trance mediumship, in Poquonock, Connecticut. Many prominent citizens from the state were present, including former governor Thomas H. Seymour. The hall was also filled with curious onlookers who watched in awe as the girl medium spoke in trance for an hour and a half. By the time Nettie was out of trance, everyone wondered how someone so young could have such extensive knowledge.

After that, she would go into trance whenever she did automatic writing or table raps and tipping. As her fame for trance mediumship grew, the teenage medium was invited to give séances throughout Connecticut and New York. Her benefactors rented space in Poquonock, Connecticut, for the trance medium along with Hartford clairvoyant physician Dr. Norton. Naturally, the inexperienced medium was filled with stage fright: "I shall never forget the sinking sensation I experienced, and how my heart palpitated in facing the sea of faces on this my first public appearance. I felt I should never become passive enough, or still the violent throbbings of my heart sufficiently to enable the unseen intelligence to obtain control. I felt the colour come and go in my cheeks, and experienced all the trepidation of stage fright that could characterize a novice for the first time facing a critical multitude."[4]

Even though Nettie was nervous, it did not affect her trance mediumship. She made a favorable impression on one gentleman from Warehouse Point, who invited her to speak the following evening. Again, she delivered a powerful trance lecture. At the close of the evening, a gentleman stepped forward. He arranged for her to lecture every other Sunday in Winsted, Connecticut. Nettie was on her way to becoming a notable trance medium. This was partly due to her spirit guide. While in trance, Nettie was under the control of the spirit of a five-hundred-year-old Aztec princess called Pinkie.

By 1861, Miss Colburn had branched out to Albany, New York. At the close of Sunday service, the congregation was abuzz with news of a disastrous battle on the banks of the Potomac. Naturally, everyone was curious about how long the conflict would continue. The spirits replied "that it would continue four years, and that it would require five practically to end it."[5] This spirit prophesied the Civil War, as the conflict came to be called, which lasted another four years.

The war also took its toll on the Colburn family. All four of Nettie's brothers enlisted. However, the spirit of Dr. Bamford assured her that all four would return home. The spirits had other messages for the medium. In August 1862, for over an hour Nettie was controlled by a group of spirits: "[T]he leading public men who had passed away from earth, but who were still interested in and guiding with care the affairs of the nation as perfectly as in their power; that it was imperatively necessary that they should communicate with President Lincoln; and they desired me to make arrangements to go to Washington and seek an immediate interview with him, assuring us that we would be well received and kindly treated; and that we should tell the President how we came to visit him, assuring us that we would have no cause to regret immediate obedience."[6]

The shy medium refused to contact President Lincoln. Despite her protests, Nettie Colburn made her way to Washington in December 1862. She was in the nation's capital to seek a furlough for her younger brother, who was gravely ill in a Union military hospital. She met with little success until she called on Mr. Cranston Laurie, an influential Spiritualist.

It was through her association with the Laurie family that Nettie was introduced to Mrs. Lincoln. The Lauries gave séances in their Georgetown home. Usually the gatherings began with old Scottish airs. According to Nettie, "Bonnie Doon" was President Lincoln's favorite song.[7]

After music, everyone joined hands, as was the custom. The medium lost consciousness and went under the control of spirit. Different guides came through, but most often it was the the spirit of old Dr. Bamford. According to Nettie, he was Lincoln's favorite and often came though when matters were urgent. "His quaint dialect, old-fashioned methods of expression, straight forwardness in arriving at his subject, together with fearlessness of utterance, recommended him as no finished style could have done."[8]

One evening, the spirit of Dr. Bamford was very concerned about the behavior of the Union troops. General Hooker had just taken command, and the soldiers were demoralized. Some even refused to obey orders. When President Lincoln asked what could be done about the situation, Dr. Bamford replied:

> *Go in person to the front; taking with you your wife and children; leaving behind your official dignity, and all manner of display. Resist the importunities of officials to accompany you, and take only such attendants as may be absolutely necessary; avoid the high grade officers, and seek the tents of the private soldiers. Inquire into their grievances; show yourself to be what you are the "Father of your People." Make them feel that you are interested in their sufferings, and that you are not unmindful of the many trials which beset them in their march through the dismal swamps, whereby both their courage and numbers have been depleted.*[9]

The other sitters at the séance were so impressed with the strength and the eloquence of her words that they forgot that Nettie was only a twenty-one-year-old woman and not a mature man.

She not only gave séances in Georgetown but also at the White House. The young woman accepted Mrs. Lincoln's invitation for a séance in December 1862 with reluctance. Later, Nettie recalled the natural trepidation of a young girl "about to enter the presence of the highest magistrate in our land, being fully impressed with the dignity of his office, and feeling that I was about to meet some superior being; and it was almost with trembling that I entered with my friends the Red Parlor at the White House, at eight, evening December 1862."[10] She had little to fear, as the president greeted her with his characteristic kindness. As he bent down to greet the petite medium, Lincoln said, with amusement, "So this is our 'little Nettie' is it, that we heard so much about?"[11]

During the séance, the spirit gave the president advice regarding the Emancipation Proclamation. The spirit spoke to him for over an hour. He was told not to delay issuing the Emancipation Proclamation—even if his cabinet was divided on the issue. The firm male voice coming from Nettie's mouth assured Abraham Lincoln that the proclamation would be the "crowning event of his administration and his life," and told him in no uncertain terms to "stand firm to his convictions and fearlessly perform the work and fulfill the mission for which he had been raised up by an overruling Providence."[12]

President Lincoln was impressed by the message from the other side. The voice of the spirit had a familiar ring and used a method of address similar to that of Daniel Webster. Lincoln later remarked to Nettie, "My child, you possess a very singular gift; but that it is of God, I have no doubt. I thank you for coming here to-night. It is more important than perhaps any one present can understand."[13]

As Nettie's access to President Lincoln and First Lady became known in Washington, D.C, she was besieged with requests to see the president. She did her best to help those in dire straits. Lincoln responded in kind. For instance, he wrote a note of introduction for the medium and her friend Anna Cosby when they wished to speak to his close associate, Joshua Speed: "My very good friend Mrs. Cosby and Miss Netty [*sic*] Colburn her friend desire an interview with you."[14] The president was pleased to learn that Speed was already well acquainted with the two ladies. "At the time, Nettie was residing at the home of her friend Anna Cosby whose husband had just lost his position as consul to Switzerland amid accusations of associating with Confederate officials while at his post in Geneva. The medium was concerned that because of her friend's fall from grace her access to the Lincoln White House would be affected."[15] In no

Abraham Lincoln, the sixteenth president of the United States. *Library of Congress.*

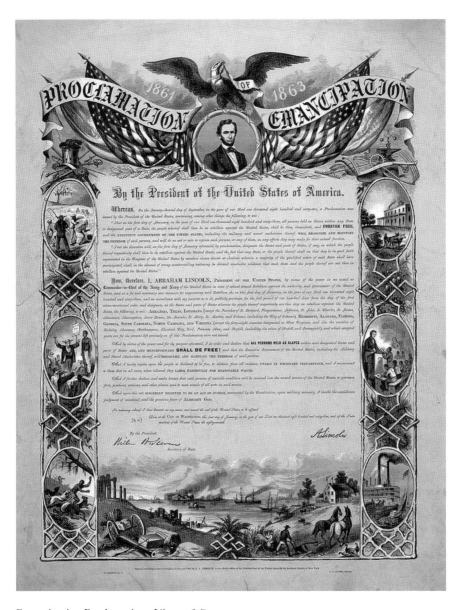

Emancipation Proclamation. *Library of Congress.*

way would Nettie wish to lose her access to the Lincolns at a time when she was pressed to plead cases for so many who were suffering.

After Lincoln's death, Nettie Colburn married N.C. Maynard and moved to White Plains, New York, where she lived for over twenty-five years. She lived a relatively quiet existence and maintained her psychic powers all her life. During the last decade of her life, she was bedridden with rheumatism. In 1890, with the help of friends, she wrote *Was Abraham Lincoln a Spiritualist?*. Francis B. Carpenter, the artist who painted the *First Reading of the Emancipation Proclamation of President Lincoln*; Melville C. Smith, a well-known gentleman from New York City; and Mark Pomeroy, a noted lawyer and writer, all agreed that Nettie Colburn was a remarkable medium and vouched for her honesty.[16]

9
A TEMPESTUOUS SPIRITUALIST

Mrs. Hooker Talks to the Spirits.
—Hartford Courant, *March 20, 1908*

There is no record of Isabella Beecher Hooker attending any of Nettie Colburn Maynard's séances; however, if she had known about the Hartford medium, she surely would have. When Belle embraced a cause, including Spiritualism, it was with her whole soul. Throughout her adult life, Belle attended séances with well-known mediums here and abroad. She particularly liked medium Victoria Woodhull and area psychics Mrs. Lazarro and Mrs. Roberts. Belle was such an ardent Spiritualist because she had witnessed a materialization: "A Laura Blibben could materialize Fred Stowe, though he did not talk through her as he did Mrs. Roberts."[1]

Also, Belle was a medium herself. When in Paris in 1874, she had a conversation with her deceased mother while lying still in her bed.[2] Sometimes the spirits used her as a medium, and she was forced to speak. For instance, "On one occasion Joan of Arc appeared to converse with her son, Ned, but Joan had great difficulty making her purpose clear in Isabella's feeble French."[3]

Isabella Beecher Hooker, however, was not born a Spiritualist; rather, she came into the world on February 22, 1822, the fifth child of Reverend Lyman Beecher, a Congregational minister, and his second wife, Harriet Porter. The family moved from their Litchfield, Connecticut residence to Boston and later Cincinnati, as Reverend Beecher was called to churches away from home. When their daughter was fifteen, the Beechers returned to Connecticut, where Belle attended the Hartford Female Seminary, a school founded by her sister Catharine.

While studying in Hartford, Belle met John Hooker. Her family would have preferred that their daughter marry a minister—however, the young law student was a descendant of Hartford's founding father, Thomas Hooker. As with his famous ancestor, Hooker was a man of principles. He believed in the abolition of slavery and had a reformist attitude toward marriage. When Isabella married Hooker in 1841, she did not immediately agree with her husband's antislavery cause but eventually supported it. For his part, Hooker sided with his wife on a woman's right to property and later shared his wife's belief in Spiritualism. There were times, though, when John was concerned about his wife's "monomania" regarding her beliefs. Isabella countered, "It was like the pot calling the kettle black."[4]

In 1853, the couple moved to Hartford, where they built a grand Gothic-style house at the corner of Forest and Hawthorn Streets on land purchased from Francis and Elisabeth Gillette. For the first twenty-five years of their marriage, Isabella focused on raising the couple's three children: Mary, born in 1845; Alice, born in 1847; and Edward, born in 1855. They were close friends with neighbors Mark Twain and his wife, Livy. Between 1871 and 1874, Twain and his family lived in the Hooker residence while the Hookers were abroad. Other neighbors included Isabella's half-sister Harriet Beecher Stowe and journalist Charles Dudley Warner.

When Belle realized that women could not legally own property once they were married, as their possessions became their husbands' property, she was livid. In 1868, she assisted in organizing the New England Woman Suffrage Association. She became a prominent speaker for women's rights and lobbied the Connecticut legislature to pass a bill to ensure a married woman's property rights. In 1877, largely thought her efforts, the Connecticut General Assembly passed a bill that gave married women the right to hold property.

Her other passion was Spiritualism, which she was introduced to when traveled to Elmira, New York, to take the water cures. Belle and her sisters Harriet and Catharine all enjoyed taking the water cures, which often afforded time away from family pressures. Water cures, or hydrotherapy treatments, were popular in the Victorian era. From 1840 to 1900, there were 213 such institutions the United States.[5] Their motto was "Wash and be healed." Advocates believed that warm and cold baths and compresses, along with drinking large amounts of water, could relieve chronic illness.

For instance, head baths were used for vertigo and hypertension, while cold showers were a tonic for melancholia. Some extreme advocates believed the water cure would treat cholera or tuberculosis or even prevent a wife from straying from her marriage.[6]

During her stay at Elmira's water cure retreat, Isabella would have heard the talk about Spiritualism and the Rochester rappings of the Fox sisters. While Rochester is one hundred miles from Elmira, both cities are part of the district of western and central New York, known as the birthplace for Mormonism and Spiritualism, as well as women's rights. Isabella was drawn to the latter two.

Belle became deeply interested in the Spiritualist cause, and she was a supporter of ardent Spiritualist Victoria Woodhull. The flamboyant stockbroker turned medium became the first woman to run for president when she was nominated by the Equal Rights Party in May 1872. Her chances of winning a national election became slimmer when she chose a black man, Frederick Douglass, as her running mate. As if that were not enough controversy, the candidate also believed in free love!

In 1872, while running for president, Victoria Woodhull was also the president of the National Society of Spiritualists. Even though she was best known for her suffrage work, Victoria Woodhull had a reputation as a talented clairvoyant and medium. Her invisible powers convinced others that the world was on the verge of becoming a single matriarchy. Isabella was thrilled by the prospect and her soon-to-be role: "The whole world would become a single matriarch, and she, Isabella Beecher Hooker of Hartford, Connecticut, was to rule as vice-regent with Christ."[7]

Not all of the Beecher family members took to Victoria Woodhull. Harriet Beecher Stowe could not stand Belle's friend. She was particularly incensed when Woodhull accused minister Henry Ward Beecher of committing adultery with one of his parishioners, Mrs. Tilton. After the attack on her beloved younger brother Henry, Harriet Beecher Stowe labeled Victoria Woodhull "a snake who should be given a good swat with a shovel."[8] She would no longer allow Isabella and John in her home. Other family members closed ranks between 1872 and 1876.

Belle sided with Victoria Woodhull and even accompanied her new friend to Europe. While in England, she attended séances conducted by a Dr. Carter, or Carterette. In 1876, Belle attended materialization séances with journalist Florence Marryat. The medium was the same doctor. His control was a little Negro girl, Rosa, who helped him to produce materialized forms of the dead. The spirits even spoke to those present: "'You must tell us your name,' said Rosa in a low voice. 'I am Janet E. Powles,'" the materialized female spirit replied. Sure enough, Isabella's friend Florence Marryat recognized the spirit as the deceased mother of her friend John Powles, even though she had only met her friend's mother on one occasion.[9]

When she returned to Hartford, Belle became obsessed with becoming a leader in the new matriarchal government. Between May 1876 and January 1877, she made several entries in her journal describing her mystical experiences and advice from spirits on the new government. She decided to have her husband, John, her nephew Fred Perkins and her daughter Mary in her cabinet.[10]

Her devotion knew no bounds. John termed her enthusiasm "monomania" and tried to monitor his wife, without much success. Belle started proselytizing. She believed it her duty to heal relatives and Nook Farm residents. She also encouraged others to develop their own mediumship. Belle particularly enjoyed giving messages to receptive Nook Farm residents.[11] For example, "In 1876, she detected in Susan Warner possibilities of 'development,' and thought of trying to materialize Beethoven, to whom Susan was devoted, so he could pass judgment on her interpretations."[12] She took it upon herself to encourage Catharine Beecher in her development of clairvoyance and healing.

By the end of 1876, Belle was ready to announce her revelations to the world. She invited her daughters Mary and Alice and their families, as well as Ned and his fiancée, in addition to the Clemenses, Gillettes and Warners, to usher in 1877. John had forbidden any mediums to attend the festivities; however, Belle issued last-minute invitations to Mrs. Perry, Mrs. Roberts., Dr. Williams and a new medium, Frank Whitmore. She assembled a group for a secret séance in the upstairs bedroom, hoping for a revelation, which, alas, did not come through. The evening ended with Mrs. Perry's daughter attacking John. It seems that the young psychic had been taken over by the spirit of an Indian warrior. Isabella's ever-patient husband was visibly upset and demanded an explanation. The next morning, when she could not come up with a good reason, John decided that his wife could not be trusted and insisted in the future she consult him before making any social arrangements.[13]

Even John Calvin Day and Henry Eugene Burton were dismayed by their mother-in-law's radical behavior. One particular upsetting incident occurred when Belle had dreamed a burglar was entering the home of Eugene Burton and severely injured him. After several false predictions, Belle was sure the time was at hand. She had everyone on high alert. John warned half the neighborhood and had two policemen ready to arrest the intruder. Everyone stayed up that night; however, no invasion occurred. While her son, Ned, remained sympathetic toward his mother, her sons-in-law were not. When Isabella predicted Burton's daughter Kathy would not live to see the New Year, he had reached his limit and forbade his mother-in-law to set foot in his house.[14]

Nevertheless, the Hookers did their best to live up to family responsibilities. For instance, when their eldest daughter married an irresponsible alcoholic, Henry Burton, they took Mary back into their home when she became ill with consumption. Isabella tried in vain to nurse her daughter back to health. After Mary died on January 20, 1886, her mother turned to Spiritualism for relief.

In October 4, 1889, Belle wrote a letter to Alice stating that she had "recently seen Mary dressed in her bridal, standing and smiling at her."[15] By 1888, Mary's father started to take a more active interest in Spiritualism and was lecturing throughout the state. He described how his friend Samuel Bowes returned to give messages, how Dr. Smith of Springfield had also returned and spoke with his characteristic stammer. Even his brother-in-law Francis Gillett gave him business advice from the other side.[16]

Her patient husband methodically took down the names of spirits that Isabella contacted through the use of the planchette. He must have been impressed to receive the names of deceased relatives and noted personalities, because he took it upon himself the keep a notebook in which jotted the names of spirits in alphabetical order. For example; listed under *B* was Lyman Beecher and listed under *N*, Napoleon.

Isabella and John Hooker celebrated their golden anniversary on August 5, 1891. According to the *New York Times*, more than two thousand invitations were sent to friends and relatives around the world.[17] While the Hartford newspapers could not bring themselves to laude Belle, the press did heap praise on her husband. The *Courant* reported on August 5, 1891, "Few come to his years who are universally valued and beloved of their fellow-men, whose influence had made so unswervingly for righteousness."[18] Mrs. Hooker was honored by a delegation of suffragists headed by Susan B. Anthony, along with many other prominent citizens. William Lloyd Garrison came down from Boston, and Thomas K. Beecher, Hartford socialite Mrs. Samuel Colt and Senator Hawley were all in attendance.[19]

The Hookers seemed to grow closer in their later years, and Belle was on better terms with her Nook Farm neighbors. However, her half-sister Harriet Beecher Stowe could not bring herself to forgive Belle for the family scandal. Neither could Mrs. Henry Ward Beecher, who would not allow Belle to attend her own brother's funeral.

In her final years, Isabella became immersed in Spiritualism, especially after the death of her "lover-husband" in 1901. She took solace in communicating with the spirit of John Hooker and that of her daughter Mary Burton, who died in 1886. In the summer of 1905, she invited Hartford medium Mrs. Lazarro to her Norfolk summer cottage, as well as Mark Twain, who often visited the area as his daughter Clara was staying at nearby sanitarium. Even though the two had their differences, particularly regarding Henry Ward Beecher's involvement with Libby Tilton, the two kept in touch.

Isabella Beecher Hooker, dressed in a gown. *Harriet Beecher Stowe Center, Hartford, Connecticut.*

Left: Isabella Beecher Hooker. *Harriet Beecher Stowe Center, Hartford, Connecticut.*

Below: Isabella Beecher Hooker and John Hooker in later years. *Harriet Beecher Stowe Center, Hartford, Connecticut.*

Twain, after all, supported the suffrage movement. He had his doubts about Spiritualism.

Never one to give in when she believed that was right, Belle sent an invitation to a séance to Mark Twain. When he expressed an investigator's skepticism, his hostess withdrew the invitation: "So I meant to invite you to talk with us in a friendly way through, our good friend who holds the key to the wicker gate. But I see you are not ready for such humble entrance, so I

Isabella with daughter Alice Hooker Day and granddaughter Katherine Seymour Day. *Harriet Beecher Stowe Center, Hartford, Connecticut.*

must withdraw my invitation for this afternoon but I am most cordially & affectionately your old friend."

Belle also made it a point to rebuke the skeptical author: "I find you are still in the attitude of most so-called 'investigators.' You know it all—but you demand through these public mediums an elucidation of the wisdom & justice of the omniscient Creator of the Universe. You have certain tests in your mind & till these are satisfied you decline to listen to the evidence."[20]

The two remained friends despite their differences. However, it was to be one of her last communications with her old Nook Farm neighbor. Isabella Beecher Hooker had a stroke on January 13, 1907, and passed to spirit twelve days later. Her funeral was conducted by three ministers, including her nephew Reverend Charles E. Stowe. Mark Twain was one of her pallbearers.[21]

Even in death, Isabella Beecher Hooker remained in the public eye; her estranged granddaughter Katherine Burton Powers sued her uncle Ned Hooker for her share of the $60,000 estate. Katherine won her case and $10,000. During the trial, the curious public heard witness Lily G. Foote, a member of Belle's Spiritualist classes, revealed Mrs. Hooker's interest in spirit communication. On March 20, 1908, the *Courant* carried this headline: "Mrs. Hooker Talks to the Spirits."[22]

Residents of the state of Connecticut still remember Isabella Beecher Hooker for her urgent appeal for women's property rights, which passed into law in 1877. Spiritualists throughout the nation, however, owe a debt of gratitude to Isabella for her passionate support of spirit communication.

MRS. SATAN COMES TO HARTFORD

To love is a right higher than constitutions or laws.
—Victoria Woodhull

Isabella Hooker's involvement in Spiritualism was fueled by her association with feminist Victoria Woodhull. The two friends could not have been more different. Belle came from an old New England family of ministers who emphasized decorum and high ideas. Victoria, on the other hand, grew up by the seat of her petticoat.

Victoria Claflin Woodhull had to be independent early in life. She was born on September 23, 1838, in Homer, Ohio. She was the seventh child of a shiftless father, Buck Claflin, and his religious wife, Roxanna. Buck was known as a con man who specialized in blackmail and schemes to sell his homemade elixirs. As a child, she did her best to avoid her father's unwanted attention and schemes. Her mother, on the other hand, claimed to have genuine healing ability and clairvoyance. She passed these gifts on to her pretty daughters, Victoria and Tennessee "Tennie."

Victoria was only too happy to accept the first marriage proposal that came her way. She met twenty-eight-year-old Dr. Canning Woodhull at a Fourth of July picnic. At the end of the day, he told the fifteen-year-old girl, "My little puss, tell your father and mother I want you for a wife."[1] While Doc was kinder to her than her abusive father, he left much to be desired as a husband. Some said that the older man tried to civilize the backwoods girl. If this was true, the good he meant his child bride was destroyed by his alcoholism and his mistress. Within weeks of their marriage, Victoria found a note in her husband's pocket: "Did you marry the child because she was en famille?" The letter was from Doc's former mistress, who was also with child.[2]

On December 31, 1854, while in Chicago, sixteen-year-old Victoria gave birth to a boy she named Byron after the poet Lord Byron. Her heart was crushed went she realized that child was mentally retarded and would never talk or behave as other children did. She could expect no help from the baby's father, as what little money Doc earned went to drink. Victoria later said of her first year of marriage, "In a single year, I grew ten years older."[3]

A few years later, on April 28, 1861, in New York, the couple had daughter, Zula. Doc quickly abandoned his wife after delivering the baby, leaving her alone and without food or medical attention. After Zula's birth, Victoria could take no more from her alcoholic, unfaithful husband. With few options she left, she turned to the spirits for assistance. Her spirit guide, Demosthenes, told her to take her children and sister Tennie and leave Dr. Woodhull.

It turned out to be a good decision for the penniless sisters. When they arrived in New York, Victoria also told anyone who cared to listen that she had powers of clairvoyance and could predict the future. She caught the attention of financier Cornelius Vanderbilt, who became a client of the young medium. Of course, Vanderbilt did not know that Victoria received some of her "predictions" from Josie Mansfield, an actress and girlfriend of Jim Fisk, Vanderbilt's competitor. While Victoria gave spiritual advice, it was her sister, Tennie, who ministered to Vanderbilt's more earthly needs. After the death of his wife, Sophia, in August 1868, the seventy-five-year-old financier asked Tennie to marry him, but she turned him down.[4] The three remained friends, though, and Vanderbilt helped the two sisters become the first women stockbrokers in 1870.

The *New York Herald* referred to Woodhull and Claflin as the "Bewitching Brokers." As Victoria became well known on Wall Street, she attracted the attention of many men, including Colonel James Harvey Blood, who served in the Sixth Missouri Infantry on the Union side during the Civil War. When she first met the Civil War veteran, she told him bluntly, "Our destinies are bound together."[5] Apparently, the dashing Blood agreed with Victoria's views on "free love," as the two moved in together.

By the time Victoria arrived in Hartford to campaign for president, she had quite the reputation. The newspapers had been quick to vilify the first woman candidate for president of the United States. She had slim support in 1872, as no one took the Equal Rights Party, which supported women's suffrage, seriously. The little support she could muster quickly evaporated when she chose Frederick Douglass, a black man, as her running mate.

The press had a field day, poking fun at the woman who would be president. None reviled her more than *Harper's Weekly*, which ran a cartoon on February 17, 1872, that left little to the imagination. The caricature by Thomas Nast was clearly aimed at Victoria Woodhull, an advocate of free love. It featured a wife carrying the burden of children and a drunken husband on her shoulders in the background. In front was a likeness of Victoria Woodhull with devil's horns in her hair. She carried a sign, "Be saved by free love." The beleaguered mother in the cartoon responded to the idea of free love by saying, "Get thee behind me, (Mrs.) Satan!" The name stuck.

Isabella Hooker's family, especially sisters Harriet and Catharine, wondered what she saw in the flamboyant woman the press had dubbed "Mrs. Satan." Rumors flew that Woodhull, a divorced woman, had a shady past. Some even claimed that she had been a prostitute. However, as a feminist she denounced prostitution, claiming even to marry for profit was nothing more than a form of prostitution. With such adverse publicity, is it any wonder that Mark Twain forbade Livy to go to Woodhull's rally when she came to Hartford to create support for the Equal Rights Party?

Things went from bad to worse for the presidential candidate. Her talk on "Principles of Social Freedom" was not well received. Crowds came more to taunt than to cheer for Victoria Woodhull. She could not even find a place to live, as she was not deemed respectable enough to stay in any hotel. In desperation, she turned to her ardent supporter and friend Isabella Beecher Hooker's brother Reverend Henry Ward Beecher for help. "Dear sir," she wrote, "I have been shut out of hotel after hotel. Now I want your assistance to be sustain[ed] at the Gilsey House from which I am now ordered out." Reverend Beecher could have intervened; however, he chose to ignore Victoria's plight, calling her complaints "whining."[6]

A sensible woman would have let the matter rest, but Victoria Woodhull was nothing if not bold. How dare he criticize her, thought Victoria. She knew for a fact the Reverend Beecher was having an affair with one of his parishioners, Elizabeth Tilton. Fellow feminist Elizabeth Cady Stanton had filled her in on the details. Theodore Tilton, a reformist newspaper editor and Beecher's close associate, was frequently away from home on the lecture circuit. Meanwhile, Mrs. Tilton sought comfort in the arms of her minister, Henry Beecher, an older man with ten grown children. When Victoria told Beecher's sisters Harriet and Catharine, they refused to believe her. However, Isabella, Henry's half-sister, believed that Victoria was telling the truth.

When Victoria Woodhull arrived for her Hartford lecture, she found the hall jammed with spectators. Many people came to ogle Mrs. Satan and jeer her talk of free love. However, Theodore Tilton introduced with great pride the woman who would speak on social freedom. He had previously written a most sympathetic biography for the newspaper *Golden Age*. In the article, "Victoria Woodhull, A Biological Sketch," Tilton lauded her skills as a social reformer and a seer.

According to Tilton, a prominent Pennsylvania judge called on him at his *Golden Age* office. The judge told the writer about Victoria Woodhull's clairvoyant powers. "Three months ago," the judge said, "while I was in New York, Mrs. Woodhull said to me, with a rush of feeling, 'Judge, I foresee that you will lose two of your children within six weeks.'" This announcement, he said, wounded him, as a tragic sort of trifling with life and death. "But," Tilton asked, "did anything follow the prophecy?" "Yes," he replied, "fulfilment; I lost two children within six weeks." The judge, who was a Methodist, thought that Victoria the clairvoyant was like "Anna the prophetess."[7]

However warm Theodore Tilton's introduction, the crowd gathered to hear Victoria Woodhull was skeptical. They listened while the speaker patiently outlined her political views, but there was little interest in the prepared speech. Undeterred by the mood of the audience, she read her eloquent plea for women's rights and social justice:

> *To love is a right higher than constitutions or laws. It is a right which constitutions and laws can neither give nor take, and with which they have nothing whatever to do, since in its very nature it is forever independent of both constitutions and laws, and exists—comes and goes—in spite of them. Governments might just as well assume to determine how people shall exercise their right to think or to say that they shall not think at all, as to assume to determine that they shall not love, or how they may love, or that they shall love.*[8]

When she came to the end, a man shouted, "Are you a free lover?" "Yes!" she replied. "I am a free lover!" And as cheers, hoots and howls redoubled, she persisted with fervor, ignoring her prepared text completely: "I have an inalienable, constitutional, and natural right to love whom I may, to love as long or as a short a period as I can, to change that love every day if I please!"[9] Undaunted, she continued to speak for another ten minutes, but the boos and jeers drummed out any words she spoke.

Why Tilton vouched for Victoria Woodhull is a mystery. Surely he knew about Beecher and his wife's affair, as he heard friends whisper the details in Hartford parlors. Even so, the affair would have remained a private matter if not for Victoria Woodhull. After having been vilified in the press for her support of free love, she took it upon herself to devote an issue of *Woodhull & Claflin's Weekly* (November 2, 1872) to the alleged adulterous affair between

Cabinet card of Victoria Woodhull. *Mathew Brady.*

Caricature of American suffragist Victoria Woodhull (1838–1927) by Thomas Nast (1840–1902). "Get thee behind me, (Mrs.) Satan!" *Library of Congress.*

Elizabeth Tilton and Reverend Henry Ward Beecher. All this took place just days before the presidential election was to be held. Anthony Comstock immediately had Woodhull; her second husband, Colonel James Blood; and her sister, Tennie C. Claflin, arrested on charges of "publishing an obscene newspaper." Her arrest, only days before the election, crushed any hope of Hull's receiving electoral votes. Regrettably, the first woman to run for president spent election day in jail.[10]

While Henry and his wife remained together, the Tiltons eventually divorced. When the scandal became public, Theodore Tilton believed he had no choice but to sue Henry Beech for alienation of affection, which he did in 1875. The trial, which captured national attention, ended in a hung jury.

After the trial, Theodore Tilton abandoned his family to spend the rest of his life in Paris. Libby was left in America with the couple's children. When she became blind, she was forced to turn to charity offered by a Spiritualist organization for support of their four children. Encouraged by the Spiritualists, Libby Tilton eventually confessed to her affair with Reverend Henry Beecher, who continued to deny his adultery.

As for Victoria Claflin Woodhull Blood, she married for a third time in 1883.[11] Her marriage to wealthy English banker John Biddulph Martin was a happy one, despite his aristocratic family's disapproval of the match. When her husband died in 1901, Victoria retired to her country estate. At her death, she left her fortune to her Zula, who cared for her brother until his death in 1932. Zula, who never married, left no heirs when she died in 1940. As requested in Victoria Woodhull Martin's will, the remaining estate was given to the Society for Psychical Research.

11

MARK TWAIN AND THE SPIRITS

I am silent on the subject because of necessity. I have friends in both places.[1]
—Mark Twain, on the afterlife

As might be expected, Mark Twain took a humorous approach to the spirit world. He loved to make fun of mediums, yet he had some of his own psychic experiences. While he was not as gifted a medium as Daniel Dunglas Home, he did have a touch of prophecy. Twain, who was born November 30, 1835, just after Halley's Comet, predicted that he would "go out with it." The day the comet returned, April 21, 1910, Mark Twain met his maker.

Samuel Langhorne Clemens, known widely by his nom de plume Mark Twain, spent his happiest years in Hartford, where his three daughters, Susy, Clara and Jean, were born. His Hartford years were also his most productive years. During his stay in Hartford, Twain wrote *The Adventures of Tom Sawyer* (1876), *Life on the Mississippi* (1883), *Huckleberry Finn* (1884), *The Prince and the Pauper* (1881) and *A Connecticut Yankee in King Arthur's Court* (1889).

For the next seventeen years (1874–1891), Mark Twain; his wife, Livy; and their three daughters lived in the Hartford home. From all accounts, Mark Twain was an affectionate father who loved to put on plays with his children. He found a literary companion in his oldest daughter. Susy loved to write and was an inspiration for Mark Twain's Joan of Arc. She also wrote her own biography of her father, published as *Papa: An Intimate Biography of Mark Twain*. Her father was inconsolable when Susy died of spinal meningitis at age twenty-four on August 18, 1896.

At the time Mark Twain and his family lived in Hartford, the city boasted the highest per-capita income of any city in the United States. One of the wealthiest states in the Union, Connecticut was known world over for the manufacture of clocks in Waterbury, hardware and tools produced by the Stanley Corporation in New Britain and fine thread milling machines invented by Francis A. Pratt and Amos Whitney in 1865. High-quality firearms—chief among them the Colt revolver—put the city on the national map. The Colt single-action revolver was unique with its interchangeable parts. Colt pistols were used during the Civil War and later became known as the "gun that won the West."

Eventually, Hartford became recognized not only as "arsenal of democracy" but also as the insurance capital of America. The three insurance giants—Hartford Fire, Aetna and Phoenix—paid in full all claims from the 1871 Chicago fire. However, the Hartford Fire Insurance Company, founded in 1810, barely survived in 1835. After a fierce fire destroyed New York's financial district that year, the company's president, Eliphalet Terry, used his personal wealth to cover damage claims.[2]

In 1871, Hartford's main attraction for Mark Twain was not guns or insurance but the city's vibrant publishing industry. When Twain first came to the city, it had twelve publishing houses. Here Twain made the acquaintance of publisher Elisha Bliss Jr. of the American Publishing Company and later *Hartford Courant* publisher Charles Dudley Warner.

In 1873, Twain commissioned architect Edward Tuckerman Potter to design a Victorian Gothic Revival house at 351 Farmington Avenue. Even though the house was not quite complete, the family moved into the twenty-five-room home on September 19, 1874. The elaborate house cost a small fortune: between $40,000 and $45,000. For Twain, it was worth it. He was sentimental about his home: "To us our house had a heart, and a soul, and eyes to see us with; and approvals and solicitudes and deep sympathies; it was of us, and we were in its confidence and lived in its grace and in the peace of its benediction."[3]

The family lived in an exclusive area on the western edge of Hartford known as Nook Farm. The neighborhood attracted politicians, painters, writers, feminists and Spiritualists. Neighbors such as Harriet Beecher Stowe, William Gillette and Isabella Beecher Hooker worked in their own ways to make a positive difference in the world. Twain was to make his mark with his writing.

His most famous neighbor was Harriet Beecher Stowe, the author of *Uncle Tom's Cabin*. Both she and her half-sister were interested in Spiritualism; Twain was no stranger to the subject.

When he was growing up in Hannibal, Missouri, just outside town lived a farmer's wife with a healing gift. She had the power to cure toothaches. "She would place her hand on the victim's jaw and then shout the word 'Believe!' The toothache would be instantly cured. Twain was present on two different occasions when such miracles were performed—both of them involved his own mother."[4]

Even so, he often found Spiritualists amusing. When Mark Twain was a reporter in California for the *Territorial Enterprise* in January 1866, he covered a séance by Ada Foye. The famous medium drew large crowds of four hundred or more eager to see her go into trance and hear the spirit raps. While the medium was in trance, her hand would write the name of the spirit present. Then raps would be heard. According to Twain's account, a spirit rapped and gave the name of John Smith: "God bless me. I believe all the dead and damned John Smiths between hell and San Francisco tackled that poor little table at once!"[5]

Ada Foye was not the first medium whom Twain had seen. He also visited a medium when he was a young man in New Orleans, a visit that may have shaped his opinion on Foye. This medium, Madame Caprell, used clairvoyance to contact the spirits. Her handbills, which she distributed liberally throughout the city, promised "to tell the future and contact a 'spiritual physician' who locates all invisible diseases, and prescribes the proper remedies for a fee of two dollars." Twain found the medium attractive: "She is a very pleasant little lady—rather pretty—about 28—say 5 feet 2¼—would weigh 116—has black eyes and hair—is polite and intelligent—uses good language, and talks much faster than I do." She predicted her client would marry twice and have ten children. In fact he married once and had four children. In at least one prediction, however, the seer was eerily prescient. "You have written a great deal," she said, "you write well—but you are rather out of practice; no matter—you will be in practice someday."[6] The last prophecy turned out to be true, even though the prediction of literary distinction was not warranted at the time. Twain, by the way, found the whole incident diverting—not unlike going to the opera.

Twain, however, took a psychic dream more seriously, as it foreshadowed his younger brother's death. The dream was to haunt him for the rest of his life. In May 1858, Twain was a riverboat pilot on the Mississippi. His brother Henry signed on to work as a "mud clerk," shoveling coal in the boiler room. Twain got into a fight with the captain and was put ashore, but Henry remained on the boat. Mark Twain reported in his journal, "[In] the morning, when I awoke I had been dreaming, and the dream was so vivid, so like reality, that it deceived me, and I thought it was real. In the dream I had seen Henry a corpse. He lay in a metallic [burial case]. He was dressed in a suit of my clothing, and on his breast lay a great bouquet of flowers, mainly white roses, with a red rose in the [centre]. The casket stood upon a couple of chairs."[7]

Soon after this dream, the boiler that Henry was tending on the riverboat *Pennsylvania* exploded. Several young men, including Henry, were killed. Twain had the duty of identifying the body of his younger brother. When he entered the "dead-room" of the Memphis Exchange on June 21, 1858, he was stunned to see his dead brother dressed in Twain's suit and laid out just like in the dream, save one detail. "I recognized instantly that my dream of several weeks before was here exactly reproduced, so far as these details went—and I think I missed one [detail] but that one was immediately supplied, for just then an elderly lady entered the place with a large bouquet consisting mainly of white roses, and in the [centre] of it was a red rose, and she laid it on his breast."[8]

Olivia "Livy" Langdon Clemens had a more favorable opinion of Spiritualists, as she had been healed by a faith healer, Dr. James R. Newton, while a teenager. Her husband loved to tell the story of how the doctor had pulled back the shades to let light into the room for the first time in two years and said, "Now we will sit up, my child." Livy then got out of her sickbed to walk a few steps.[9]

The husband and wife were opposites in many ways. Olivia, ten years younger than her spouse, came from a privileged background in Elmira, New York. Her father, a wealthy merchant, even provided the couple with luxurious home as a wedding present. Her husband-to-be grew up in Hannibal, Missouri, the son of a widow. Twain's father, a judge, died when he was eleven. Early on, Mark Twain had to fend for himself. He took an apprenticeship with a printer and then became a riverboat pilot on the Mississippi River before heading west to Nevada to try his hand at mining. He ended up a journalist for the Virginia City, Nevada *Territorial Enterprise*.

By the time the two were married on February 2, 1870, Twain was ready to settle down. He affectionately called his bride Livy, and she called him Youth. They remained compatible for thirty-four years of marriage. His wife often served as editor and advisor.

They had four children. As was an all-too-frequent occurrence in Victorian times, two of their offspring died early. Their first child, a son named Langdon, died at nineteen months from diphtheria, and their second, Susy, died in 1896 from spinal meningitis in their Hartford residence. The

Left: Mark Twain. *Library of Congress.*

Below: Mark Twain and his daughter Susy. *Mark Twain House and Museum, Hartford, Connecticut.*

couple tried to make contact with their deceased daughter, Susy, in 1900: "Staying at a cottage at Saranac Lake, New York, they took one of their daughter's brooches to a medium who said Susie [*sic*] wanted a biography she had written of her father to be published."[10] Soon after the session, Mark Twain sold his Hartford home, which the family no longer used but kept in memory of Susy.

Not surprisingly, Livy was a close friend to Isabella Beecher Hooker, an ardent Spiritualist. Much to Livy's husband's dismay, the couple attended a séance at the Hooker home on New Year's Eve. Apparently, the spirit of an Indian chief took over Isabella's body: "At one point she came flying down the stairs with a tomahawk!" She believed she was the embodiment of an Indian chief—she was never a warrior, she was a chief—and at that point, Mark Twain turned to Livy and said, 'Okay, that's it—we're going. Too weird.'"[11]

One wonders if Twain had Belle in mind when he ridiculed amateur mediums in his unpublished story "Schoolhouse Hill." He is skeptical of a Spiritualist who believes she is in contact with the spirit of Lord Byron:

Mark Twain House, Hartford, Connecticut. *Photograph by the author.*

It was Lord Byron's spirit. Byron was the most active poet on the other side of the grave in those days, and the hardest one for a medium to get rid of. He would reel off rods of poetry now, of his usual spirit pattern—rhymy [sic], jingly, and all that, but not that good, for his mind had decayed since he died. At the end of the three-quarters of an hour, he went away to hunt for a word that would rhyme with silver—good luck and good riddance.[12]

Later in life, Twain had a brush with the paranormal that may have changed his mind about the spirits. In 1908, Twain, now a widower, was playing billiards with his friend and biographer Albert Bigelow Paine. When they left the pool table, there were two red and two white balls. The next morning, they found the two red balls, but only one white ball. Despite a thorough search, they could not find the missing white ball. After playing for a short interval, Mark Twain reached in his pocket for a white ball he had placed there. When he placed it on the pool table, he was surprised to see there were now three white balls on the table.

Paine suggested that the incident may have been prank by a mischievous spirit. Perhaps the spirit dematerialized one white ball. Twain replied, "Yes, if one of us were a medium that might be considered an explanation." After giving the matter some thought, Mark Twain said, "Well it happened. That's all I can say, and no one can ever convince me that it didn't."[13]

12

SPIRITUAL MANIFESTATIONS

For the most part, these phantoms were agreeable to me, and filled me with a dreamy delight.
—Charles Beecher

In contrast to Mark Twain's casual dismissal of the spirits, the Reverend Charles Beeecher was a true believer. Even as child, he had seen spirits in his bedroom. After his mother tucked young Charles into his bed, he would keep his eyes wide open. Often, he witnessed a palpitating crowd of faces and forms before his young eyes. He was not afraid of the spirits present, as he explained, "For the most part, these phantoms were agreeable to me, and filled me with a dreamy delight."[1] Sometimes he saw an old white-haired gentleman playing the violin, accompanied by a tall woman in dressed in an unusual costume with a high-collared fur cape. The woman danced in time to the music the gentleman played. Of couse, when Charles told his mother of his visititations, she was quick to correct his impressions, telling the sensitive boy that there was no one in the room.

Charles Beecher was born to a Christian family in Litchfield, Connecticut. He was the son of Lyman Beecher and Roxana Foote Beecher. His siblings included author Harriet Beecher Stowe, minister Henry Ward Beecher and educator Catharine Beecher. Of the three, he was the closest to Harriet. When his sister and her minister husband moved to Florida a year after the Civil War, he joined the couple. From 1871 to 1873, Charles Beecher was the state superintendent of public instruction in Florida. He was also a prolific writer and wrote several books on religion:

The Incarnation, or, Pictures of the Virgin and Her Son (1849)
The Duty of Disobedience to Wicked Laws (1851)
David and His Throne (1855)
Pen Pictures of the Bible (1855)
The Life of David King of Israel (1861)
Autobiography, Correspondence, etc. of Lyman Beecher (1863)
Redeemer and Redeemed (1864)
Spiritual Manifestations (1879)
The Eden Tableau, or, Object Bible-Teaching (1880)
Patmos; or, the Unveiling (1896)

Beecher was interested in both traditional Christianity and Spiritualism. In April 1858, he gave a report to the Congregational Association of New York and Brooklyn on what he termed "spiritual manifestations." The report began with this premise: "In every soul, there is an invisible realm, a heavens and earth of thought, a universe within."[2] Revolutionary in its day for a Spiritualist view of Christainity, the report was subsequently published by Lee and Shephard Publishers.

Congregationalists may not have been ready for Beecher's brand of spirituality. For example, the minister was so enthusiastic about mediumship development that he compared the Spiritualist circle to that of family prayer in Christian households. Even though directions for development are not given in the mainstream presses, the spirits gave their own advice: "Directions are given for from within such circle, and in one out every four families, it is said a medium will be found."[3]

While he was receptive to spirit communication, Charles Beecher was not oblivious to its pitfalls. He mentions that there are "spheres, grades or ranks in the spirit world."[4] He further explains, "Communications and revelations we receive are reliable and good in proportion as they emanate from spirits of higher spheres and commend themselves to our reason and conscience."[5]

He also states that there are three general classifications of spirits: "celestrial above matter, terrestrial in matter, and substerrestrial beneath matter."[6] While the prophets and apostles of Christ were mediums of the highest order, the average person needs to be aware of the possibility of higher and lower realms of heavenly, earthy and hellish spirits.

Beecher cited the spirit that plagued the Phelps home in Stratford (see chapter 4) as an example of those from the lower element. Even though Reverend Phelps seemed sincere in his belief, his faith was greately tested by the poltergeist activity in 1850–1851. How could he not be affected by the raps, voices and strange activity? Spoons, turnips and even knives were thrown by invisible hands. These were clearly the actions of a malicious spirit.

Apparently, the good man had brought other spirits of a more helpful connection. For instance, on one occasion, he learned through a series of raps that the brother of Mrs. Phelps was unhappy on the other side because he felt that his sister had been treated unfairly in the settlement of an estate by a person with the initials D.S. When Reverend Phelps investigated the matter, he found the spirit of his brother-in-law to be correct. "He found evidence sufficient to confirm suspicion of fraud, excited by the communications, but nothing sufficient to convict in a court of justice."[7]

Most of the other communications seemed to be petty. For instance, when Reverend Phelps asked, "What do you want?" a spirit replied, "A piece of pumpkin pie."[8] Another spirit had the nerve to request a glass of gin![9] Apparently earthly desire is not diminished by death.

At times, though, the spirits could be dangerous. The two young children became the target of the spirits' abuse. For example, Anna, the reverend's stepdaughter, was slapped by invisible hands. Her parents often saw red marks appear on her skin. According to the editor of the *Bridgeport Standard*, the child nearly died when a pillow was reportedly pressed over her head while she was asleep.[10] Her brother Henry was also attacked by invisible forces that punched the boy and even attempted to carry him from his bed: "A newspaper reporter claimed that he once saw the boy carried from this bed by an invisible force and dumped on the floor. In front of a number of witnesses, he was once lifted into the air so high that his hair brushed the ceiling of the room."[11]

Not all spirits are malevolent. As Reverend Beecher points out, some spirits are of a benign nature. For example, the spirits that contacted his sister Harriet Beecher Stowe were of a helpful nature. The author of *Uncle Tom's Cabin* made contact with the author of *Jane Eyre*, Charlotte Brontë. The English novelist (April 21, 1815–March 31, 1855) was eldest of the three Brontë sisters. Mrs. Stowe used a private medium who communicated with a planchette. Stowe asked her spirit friend mundane questions about the spirit world such as, "Are those who are beautiful in this world, beautful there?" To which the purported spirit of Charlotte Brontë replied, "Yes, but the degree of spiritual beauty here makes the truest beauty with us.'"[12] She also asked the question, "Is there time in the spirit world?" The answer? "No, a thousand years are but a moment."[13]

She then moved on to evidential questions.

> *When were you born?*
> *April 1816*
> *When did you leave this world?*
> *March 1855*[14]

While conversations with deceased writers may be interesting, they are still of an earthly nature. According to Beecher, the highest class of phenomena is that of conversations with Jesus. One gentleman related such an encounter that took place in the back room of a law office. Acccording to the man's account, "I met the Lord Jesus Christ face to face."[15] He appeared "like any other man." Immediately, the man bowed down before Jesus and wept at his feet. When he later sat down by the fire, he received "a mighty baptism by the Holy Ghost."[16]

According to Charles Beecher, Jesus came to heal and cast out negative spirits:

> *He commenced at once healing diseases and casting out evil spirits (one prolific cause of disease) and sent out the twelve and seventy to do the same. Jesus prayed only to God Almighty, and rebuked spirits of a lower nature. He would not tolerate spirits of a lower nature. Jesus sought only the highest spirits.*

Beecher cites the transfiguration in the Bible as an example of this. Here, the spirits of Elijah and Moses appeared and God spoke to Jesus:

> *After six days Jesus took with him Peter, James and John the brother of James, and led them up a high mountain by themselves. There he was transfigured before them. His face shone like the sun, and his clothes became as white as the light. Just then there appeared before them Moses and Elijah, talking with Jesus. Peter said to Jesus, "Lord, it is good for us to be here. If you wish, I will put up three shelters—one for you, one for Moses and one for Elijah." While he was still speaking, a bright cloud covered them, and a voice from the cloud said, "This is my Son, whom I love; with him I am well pleased. Listen to him!"*[17]

Children of Reverend Lyman Beecher; Charles Beecher is in the back row, second to the right. *Harriet Beecher Stowe Center, Hartford, Connecticut.*

Beecher's book received a favorable review from Samuel Byron Brittan. However, he was critical of Reverend Beecher's definition of sin, which Spiritualists define as "immaturity in development." Brittan explained, "We believe that the theological, philosophical, and ethical writers agreeing defining sin in general terms to be the commission of some manifest wrong or neglect of an obvious duty in the manner which implies the exercise of choice of the individual and the exercise of voluntary powers."[18]

Brittan also disagreed with Charles Beecher on the character of spirits. He cautioned readers to use care in discerning spirits: "The gift of discerning spirits is possessed and exercised by many persons, others who have scarcely acquired ordinary freedom in the use of their vernacular, yet speak in various and foreign languages; the ignorant utter new ideas, and unskilled hands exercise delicate and difficult works of art—execute them without powers of thought or action of the individual will."[19] He ends the review with a quote from Jesus: "We insist that the real character of the spirit is most clearly revealed by what they do and say, and the declaration of Christ, on this point is the law of nature: 'Wherefore by their fruits shall ye know them.'"[20] Thus Brittan concluded his review of *Spiritual Manifestations*, deeming it a book worthy of serious study.

PATRONESS TO THE SPIRITS

Why, this body isn't me.
—nine-year-old Theodate Pope

Theodate Pope would have agreed with Reverend Charles Beecher on the merits of Spiritualism. She, too, believed that spirit communication was worthy of serious study. In fact, parapsychology was a lifelong interest of Theodate Pope Riddle. She often invited Dr. William James to her home. The popular guest was a noted psychologist and author of *Varieties of Religious Experiences*. She was also interested in architecture, art and philanthropy.

The generous Farmington resident was born on February 2, 1868. The only child of industrialist Alfred Atmore Pope and his wife, Ada Lunette Brooks, she was christened Effie Brooks Pope, much to her dismay. When she was twelve, Effie rebelled and insisted that her parents change her name to Theodate in honor of her grandmother Theodate Stackpole.

Perhaps it was because she was often left alone in the care of governesses and maids that Theo became quite sensitive to her inner life. At nine, she had an out-of-body episode that convinced her that there was more to life than met the eye. It happened while she was sitting on the stairs quietly listening to her mother talking with the seamstress. She quickly realized that she was not in her body. Then she heard a voice say, "Why, this body isn't me."[1]

Her parents decided to send their independent daughter to Miss Porter's School for Young Ladies in Farmington, Connecticut. It turned out to be a good match, as the teenager loved the country atmosphere and made friends with many of her fellow students, including Mary Hillard, who became a lifelong friend. They often read the Bible aloud and discussed the meaning of passages.[2]

Mary was also interested in Spiritualism. Theodate, who had had an out-of-body experience, listened with rapt attention to her friend's accounts of spirit communication.By the end of the nineteenth century, the Populist movement was being taken more seriously by the academic community. In the United States, Professor William James arranged many séances with the Boston trance medium Lenore Piper.

In 1904, after the death of John Hillard, Theo and John's sister Mary made a visit to a Mrs. Piper in Boston. They were introduced to the medium as "Miss Smith" and "Miss Bergman." Mrs. Piper went into trance and picked up a pencil to write message from her two guides—the Imperator and the Rector. While the spirit guides did their best to communicate with John's spirit, Theodate remained skeptical. At one point, Theo said to the purported spirit of her dead friend, "Tell him he was always a dear fellow, but he didn't used to be as stupid as he is now."[3]

After a rocky start, more intelligent and evidential messages came through the Rector. For example, John told Theo the name of the janitor at Andover School, which he had attended as a boy. No one in the room would have had access to this information—especially the medium.John continued to advise his friend on subsequent séances. He also cautioned her about visiting other mediums, who might be "unclean in mind and body."[4]

Many people, including suffragettes such as Susan B. Anthony and Charlotte Perkins Gilman, embraced the principles of Spiritualism, which advocated a less restrictive life for women. Adherents believed unwanted pregnancies and loveless marriages were the cause of many maladies. For instance, to overcome depression, Spiritualists recommended that women loosen their corsets and get plenty of fresh air, healthy food and exercise. As Theodate became more familiar with the tenets of Spiritualism, she took up bicycling two or three miles a day and eating lots of bread, cheese, parsley and lettuce. Not only did she become healthier, but her ambitions also increased. She was now interested in pursuing a career in architecture.[5]

After her education at Miss Porter's School in Farmington, Theodate took a grand tour of Europe, where she studied European architecture. In 1901, she designed Hill-Stead, a magnificent home for her parents. Both were delighted. Her father hung his favorite French Impressionists paintings of Manet, Degas and Monet in his new residence, while her mother was equally pleased with its spacious rooms for entertaining.

Eventually, Hill-Stead became her home, where she entertained many honored guests, including Richard Hodgson, Katharine Hepburn, Mary Cassatt, William James and his brother, novelist Henry James. According to Theodate's goddaughter, Phyllis Fenn Cunningham, Henry James spent happy days at Hill-Stead in the summer of 1911. The sixty-eight-year-old novelist appreciated the French Impressionist paintings and the magnificent sunken garden.

Henry James may have been the brother of Professor William James, but the two had very divergent tastes. Henry loved luxury and refinement and thought séances were "dull and repulsive." Henry particularly objected to the class of people that séances attracted. Brother William, a founding member of the American Society for Psychical Research, was very much of the opposite persuasion. He was fascinated by altered states of consciousness and became a lead investigator of Boston medium Lenore Piper. The Harvard University professor had his first sitting with Piper in 1885, the year after the death of his young son. After several sessions with the trance medium, James became convinced that she received information from supernatural sources. Dr. James quipped, "If you wish to upset the law that all crows are black, it is enough if you prove that one crow is white. My white crow is Mrs. Piper."[6]

Theodate Pope was a generous contributor to William James's research on mediumship. Her interest in life after death intensified after the death of her father in 1913. She was particularly intent on creating a society in Hartford for the study of parapsychology similar to the Society for Psychical Research (SPR) in London. The nonprofit organization established in 1882 in the United Kingdom stated its purpose as understanding "events and abilities commonly described as psychic or paranormal by promoting and supporting important research in this area" and to "examine allegedly paranormal phenomena in a scientific and unbiased way."[7]

In the spring of 1915, she decided to go to England to visit the SPR. When she boarded RMS *Lusitania* on May 1 that year, this vision of a Connecticut parapsychology foundation was foremost in her mind. The first-class passenger was accompanied by her maid, Emily Robinson, and Professor Edwin Friend. He and his wife, Marjorie, were expecting their first child. Even though his wife was disappointed that she could not make the journey, she was happy to know that her husband and Miss Pope would be guests of England's leading Spiritualist, Sir Oliver Lodge.

The couple was very interested in mediumship and parapsychology research. In 1913, Edwin Friend, a recent graduate of Harvard University, was an assistant to Professor James Hyslop of Columbia University and president of the American Society for Psychical Research. "Friend's salary of $2,000 a year was appropriated from a donation made to the organization by one of its founders and directors, Theodate Pope."[8]

Pope, fond of Edwin and his wife, Marjorie, housed them at her country estate. She was particularly intrigued by Marjorie's budding mediumship. "With further assistance from Theodate, Friend became editor of the *Journal of the ASPR*. Hyslop sent Friend articles that were to be published, but instead, Friend opted to write articles about séances held in Farmington where Marjorie produced automatic writing while communicating with deceased members of the ASPR. Enraged that his assistant was no longer under his control, Hyslop repossessed the editorship of the *Journal of the ASPR*."[9] Both Friend and Pope resigned from the board of directors.

After such shoddy treatment in America, Theodate Pope and Edwin Friend wanted an opportunity to form a more progressive society for psychical research. However noble their motives, fate intervened in the form of a German torpedo. As the *Lusitania* entered the war zone off the coast of Ireland, the Germans attacked the vessel.

Theodate Pope and her companions were forced to jump from the balcony. She swam toward a stray oar and was able to remain afloat with the aid of the flotsam, which slid up her voluminous skirt. When she was picked up by rescuers, the unconscious woman was placed among the dead on the deck of the *Julia*. Fortunately, a fellow passenger and nurse, Belle Naish, spotted her. Theodate appeared more dead than alive. When the nurse first touched Pope's body weighed down by saltwater-soaked clothes, Naish exclaimed, "She feels like a sack of cement!"[10] However, Mrs. Naish believed that Theodate could be revived by the doctor. Thus Theodate Pope became the last of the survivors to be pulled from the icy waters. Miss Robinson and Professor Friend were not as fortunate.

Theodate Pope wondered why she survived when 1,198 passengers drowned that day. She was particularly puzzled, as she told her friends, "I truly believe there was no one on the ship who valued life as little as I do." The ordeal was to scar her for life. She avoided travel by water and was plagued by frequent nightmares. Often she could not get to sleep until 3:00 a.m.[11]

As for Marjorie Friend, the grief-stricken widow made contact with her husband within weeks of his death. According to medium May Pepper Vanderbilt, "The only thing really surprising thing about the message was that it came so soon after Professor Friend's death. Then too you must remember that Professor Friend had made long studies of the occult and knew the rules of communication."[12] Friend's message was a much-needed comfort to his very pregnant wife, who later gave birth to a baby girl on September 22, 1915. Sadly, the child, whom she named Faith, was born mentally retarded.

Almost a year to the day of her rescue, on May 6, 1916, Theodate Pope surprised everyone by marrying for the first time at age forty-nine. Her new husband, John Wallace Riddle, had been an ambassador to Russia under President Theodore Roosevelt. In 1920, John was appointed ambassador to Argentina. She stayed with her new husband for a few months but then returned to Farmington to oversee construction of Avon School for Boys in Connecticut. She was partially motivated to build an ideal school for boys because she had adopted three orphans. The first, Gordon Brockway, died at age four after a bout with polio. Her two other foster sons, Paul Martin and Donald Carson, lived to enjoy an idyllic childhood at Hill-Stead. Paul eventually settled in Springfield, Massachusetts, while Donald moved to California. Their affectionate mother missed their lively presence when they moved on with their lives.

In addition to her generous nature, Theodate Pope Riddle was quite psychic. For instance, she was very sensitive to her goddaughter, Phyllis. Once when the teenager was depressed, her aunt sent her chauffeur, Charles, to bring Phyllis to Hill-Stead. Her goddaughter was left to wonder, "How did Aunt Theo know that I was depressed?"[13]

Theodate Pope was also sensitive to the vibrations of Hill-Stead. When she was awakened in a New York hotel by a vision of flames of the wall of her Farmington bedroom, she called her butler, Ernest, at 2:00 a.m. According to Phyllis, "Before my godmother could question him, he said 'Yes, Miss Pope, we have just put the fire out in the wastepaper basket!'"[14]

Theodate Pope Riddle spent her last years at Hill-Stead. Her idyllic life was marred by the death of her devoted husband, John Riddle, who passed in 1941. However, she continued to oversee Avon Old Farms School and entertain visitors at Hill-Stead. When she passed to spirit in 1946, she requested that she be buried in her beloved sunken garden beside her favorite pine tree.

Theodate Pope Riddle was as generous in death as she was in life. She bequeathed $100,000 to each of her adoptive sons and left $400,000 in a trust to maintain Hill-Stead. Today, her nineteen-room home is a museum filled with the finest paintings by Eugenie Carriere, Mary Cassatt, Edgar Degas, Édouard Manet, Claude Monet and James McNeill Whistler and

Left: Theodate Pope at the time of her rescue from the *Lusitania*. *Hill-Stead Museum archives, Farmington, Connecticut.*

Below: RMS *Lusitania*. *Library of Congress.*

Above: Hill-Stead, west façade, 1905. *Hill-Stead Museum archives, Farmington, Connecticut.*

Right: Professor William James. *Houghton Library, Harvard University.*

engravings by Albrecht Dürer. If visitors look closely at her library, they will note that it is filled with volumes on parapsychology. Theodate Pope Riddle never lost interest in the paranormal.

PINE GROVE SPIRITUALIST CAMP

*We affirm that communication with the so-called dead is a fact, scientifically
proven by the phenomena of Spiritualism.*
—Declaration of Principles, National Spiritualist Association of Churches

The publication of books such as William James's *The Varieties of Religious
Experience* and Charles Beecher's *Spiritual Manifestations* opened the
eyes of Connecticut readers to the presence of a spiritual universe. Many
became convinced that the material universe was a representation of divine
thought. As movements such as New Thought, Theosophy and Spiritualism
challenged traditional ideas, citizens became increasingly interested in the
world beyond the material veil.

By 1861, Connecticut had mediums registered with their specialties.
Some, such as physical mediums, produced raps, and other mediums
communicated with spirit by clairvoyance, writing or trance. Still others
were known for magnetic healing. Here is partial record of the mediums
of the day: "L. Kinney, S. Miller, Mrs. Guile, and Thompson. Raps—Miss
F. Jordan, New Boston. Writing—Sarah Dearth, Thompson; Mrs. Pettis,
Putnam; W. Keith, Mrs. N.A. Keith, healing, etc.—Tolland."[1]

The 1880 census listed occupations of clairvoyant, spirit medium,
psychometrist, trance lecturer and magnetic healer. Some, such as thirty-seven-
year-old Mary Wright of New Haven, Connecticut, were willing to go public,
while other individuals preferred to keep their work private.[2] Those who did
advertise used local newspapers or Spiritualist presses such as the *Banner of Light*.

As their numbers grew, Spiritualists scouted for places to share their philosophy with like-minded people. They wanted a quiet spot, away from the skeptical eyes of nonbelievers. With this thought in mind, three Spiritualist families looked for a place close to the ocean. In the 1880s, they purchased forty acres on a peninsula between Smith Cove and the Niantic River for $1,000. The area known as Pine Grove had space enough for 350 pine-treed plots of land, each measuring twenty-five by fifty feet. At first, the believers pitched tents to attend religious revival meetings. Later, they built Gothic-style cottages with gingerbread trim.[3] At one point, there were more than one hundred such houses at the camp. Visitors welcomed the opportunity to escape the heat of the city and commune with nature.

As Nettie Pease Fox wrote in 1879, the camps provided an opportunity for "social intercourse . . . Spiritualist and liberalist from different parts of the country are brought together, become acquainted, and plans can be matured for the spread of spiritual teachings."[4] Spiritual seekers enjoyed hearing messages from local mediums, many of whom had American Indian, Hindu and other exotic guides. It was a world away from everyday reality.

The Spiritualists believed in having a good time as well as being guided by spirits. They added an amphitheater, dance hall pavilion and a refreshment stand, as well as well an area for roller skating and even a sightseeing observation tower. In its heyday, "as many as five hundred horses and carriages arrived to attend outdoor Sunday services," according to the Reverend Henrietta L. Cox, past president of the Ladies Aid Society, the group in charge of Pine Grove Spiritualist Camp.[5]

Among those who enjoyed the summer services at Pine Grove in 1894 were Lieutenant Cornelius Ryan of the Hartford police, his son D.F. Ryan of Hartford's *Telegram* and Edward J. Ryan, a professor at Saint Mary's College in Maryland. On Sunday, August 14, they listened with rapt attention to Edgar W. Emerson as he gave communications from the other side of life. Those who were fortunate to receive a message from spirits quickly recognized the names given.[6]

Of course, not everyone who attended meetings were Spiritualists. People of all creeds were welcome, and many came with their families. Children took off their shoes and played happily, while adults enjoyed the cool ocean breezes. Some simply came for entertainment. Dances were held twice a week in the pavilion and socials on Tuesday, Wednesday, Thursday and Saturday evenings. Soldiers stationed nearby stopped by for the dancing and socials.[7]

As more people joined the Spiritualist movement, the time was ripe for a state organization. In March 1883, the Connecticut Spiritualist Association was founded. It held its first convention a few years later. Each year, more and more people wished to attend. At its fifteenth anniversary, it held a two-day convention on May 6, 1901, at Unity Hall in Hartford—over three hundred people had to be turned away.

People were more than willing to pay ten cents to hear populist orator Mary Elizabeth Lease. She had become famous when she advised Kansas farmers to "raise less corn and more hell." She also supported the suffrage movement, as well as temperance. However, by 1896, she was less interested in politics and more interested in life after death. Her topic at the Spiritualist convention was "If a Man Die, Shall He Live Again?" Mrs. Lease explained that throughout history, many famous scholars believed life after death was possible. She cited the early Greeks and Romans, as well as Abraham and Moses, Job, David, Isaiah, Socrates, Plato, Cicero, David, Milton and Tennyson as believers in immortality. With passion in her voice, she exclaimed, "Spiritualists absolutely knew that this question of the ages has been answered in the affirmative."[8]

As attentive as the audience was to Mrs. Lease, they also came for messages delivered by Mrs. Marion Carpenter of Detroit, Michigan. She did not disappoint them. People in the convention hall were moved when the medium gave the name of "Annie" to a woman whose daughter Annie had died. She also gave the names "Frankie Smith" and "Mary." They were identified as a brother and sister in the spirit world. While no one came forward to claim the spirit who gave the name of "Paulinia W. White," a gentleman in the audience did recognize the name "George Ellebee."[9]

Interest in Spiritualism continued to grow. On May 8, 1916, the annual meeting of the state association of Spiritualists had a most enthusiastic audience. Perhaps it was because the speaker that year was noted medium Mrs. Mary Vanderbilt. According to reporters from the *Hartford Courant*, she gave a "broad scope of messages, and many of an 'unusual quality.'" For instance, "Picking up a cluster of violets, Mrs. Vanderbilt brought up the spirit of one Jabez Woodbury, accompanied by a man named Roberts who told his wife to go ahead with her writing, mentioning that a certain person had not a long time to remain here."[10] When asked about the war (World War I), the medium said, "Man's selfishness is the cause of the war. Man is drunk with the wine of greed. Did you ever think that the war would stop if the factories in this country stopped making munitions and shipping them to Europe?"[11]

Curiosity about the possibility of spirit communication only increased after World War I, as many sought to make contact with fallen soldiers and loved ones. Pine Grove Spiritualist Camp remained a popular destination. As the demand for mediums increased, training became important. During the 1920s, Spiritualism became more organized and established schools to educate mediums such as the Morris Pratt Institute in Wisconsin, the William T. Stead Center in Chicago and later the Arthur Findlay College in England. Many Connecticut mediums received their training through the Morris Pratt Institute, as well as local Spiritualist church development circles.

The 1920s were a wonderful time to be a medium in Connecticut. The decade ushered in a time of abundance for the state, which derived much of its wealth from tobacco, firearms and the manufacture of sewing machines, clocks and later typewriters. Pine Grove Spiritualist Camp benefitted as well and continued to draw visitors from New York, Rhode Island and Massachusetts. Visitors looked forward to spending a week at one of its lovely cottages. Others, such as Hartford controller Charles Robins, came only for the weekend, and many invited guests for just the day to hear the speakers.

At times, as many as two hundred people crowded the grounds to receive a message from their spirit loved ones. They also enjoyed the lovely organ music and fine orators. In 1921, speakers at Pine Grove—including Mrs. Cora Pullion of Bridgeport, Connecticut; Mrs. Mary Pilling of Springfield, Massachusetts; and Reverend Millicent Wilson of Malden, Massachusetts— attracted a good-sized crowd.[12]

Old-timers often talk about the physical mediumship that went on in the basement of the temple or in the private homes of mediums. A well-known medium in the Harford area even gave physical, or trumpet, séance. "The séance which lasted for an hour and a half, and those present witnessed spirit lights the size of an orange and heard the spirit of an American Indian beat the tom-tom. Especially evidential were the voices of the loved ones which come through the floating trumpet."[13] Spirits are said to speak through the trumpet by building up vibrations within it according to Mary Elizabeth, the editor and publisher of the *Progressive Thinker*.[14]

While some physical mediums did not wish to go public, other people such as Mrs. M.E. Cadwallader, editor and publisher of the *Progressive Thinker*, were more than willing to talk to the public about the Spiritualism. In May 1930, the Connecticut State Spiritualist Association invited Mrs. Cadwallader of Chicago to speak. "When queried on what was the problem with Spiritualist movement, she complained that mediums were not very selective in their clients. 'Anyone can secure a sitting regardless of his mental attitude,' she said, 'This spoils the efficacy of mediumship.'"[15] She advised those wishing to communicate with spirit to sit in contemplation for several hours before they visited a medium.

The second speaker that day was the Reverend William E. Hammond of Wheeling, West Virginia. He was well known in the Spiritualist community for his dynamic delivery. Billy Hammond had shared the podium with Dr. Le Roi Crandon at the 1927 Massachusetts State Spiritualist Association in Boston. At the time, Dr. Crandon's wife, Margery, was making headlines throughout the United States for her physical mediumship. Members of the Connecticut Spiritualist Association could hardly wait to hear Hammond's views on recent developments in spirit communication.

The 1930s brought a decline in attendance to Pine Grove. During the Great Depression, the camp suffered losses. When the Reverend Henrietta L. Cox first came to Pine Grove, it was thriving. Eventually, Pine Grove had to sell many of its cottages to non-Spiritualists. In the 1960s, many of the cottages were winterized for year-round use. Now about 90 percent of the 135 homes belong to year-round residents.[16] All that remains of Pine Grove

Sign for Pine Grove. *Photograph by the author.*

Pine Grove Spiritualist Camp. *Photograph by the author.*

Spiritualist Camp is a simple white wooden temple with a rather rustic interior and the parish house, a two-story Victorian cottage.

During the summer, believers from New London, Norwich, Willimantic and Newington still travel to Pine Grove. Visitors enjoy the cool breezes from Niantic Bay along with the messages from their spirit loved ones. According to Reverend Henrietta Cox, "Spiritualism is not different than other religions. We just don't accept death as final."[17]

Epilogue
MESSAGES FROM THE SPIRIT WORLD

Our Master is Reason;
Our Law is Love to Man;
Our Religion is Justice;
Our Light is Truth;
Our Structure is Association;
Our Path is Progression;
Our Works are Development;
Our Heaven is Harmony;
Our God is the Universal Father! [1]
—*Reverend Andrew Jackson Davis*

Spiritualists held very lofty sentiments regarding their fellow men, as evidenced by the above passage from Andrew Jackson Davis. He used this "Book of Life" statement to end a speech to the Harmonial Brotherhood. Many Spiritualists wished to establish a base for their religion as well as improve the lives around them—for they believed that it was possible to establish heaven on earth. When they banded together to form the Harmonial Brotherhood, the new movement chose Hartford as the site for its conference under the guidance of Andrew Jackson Davis.

Russell Perkins Ambler, a reporter for the *Spirit Messenger*, wrote, "New and important instructions have been received by Mr. A.J. Davis, in reference to the formation of a Harmonial Brotherhood, in which the sublime and beautiful principles of our Philosophy may be illustrated in practice. Being visited by a highly enlightened and advanced spirit in the Second Sphere, he is informed that the time has now arrived when an outward embodiment of the great truths of Nature should be presented to the world."[2]

Davis was also receiving dictations for his book *The Principles of Nature: Her Divine Revelations and A Voice to Mankind*. He had many enthusiastic witnesses, who saw the largely uneducated young man turn into an educated philosopher of the highest rank. Dr. George Bush, professor of Hebrew at the University of New York, declared, "Taken as a whole the work is a profound and elaborate discussion of the philosophy of the universe, and for grandeur of conception, soundness of principle, clearness of illustration, order of arrangement and encyclopedic range of subjects, I know no work of any single mind that will bear away from it the palm."[3] The book begins with Earth's beginning:

> *Matter and Power were existing as a Whole, inseparable. The Matter contained the substance to produce all suns, all worlds, and systems of worlds, throughout the immensity of Space. It contained the qualities to produce all things that are existing upon each of those worlds. The Power contained Wisdom, and Goodness, Justice, Mercy and Truth. It contained the original and essential Principle that is displayed throughout immensity of Space, controlling worlds and systems of worlds, and producing Motion, Life, Sensation and Intelligence, to be impartially disseminated upon their surfaces as ultimates.*[4]

ISABELLA BEECHER HOOKER

Spirit Writing

Isabella Beecher Hooker was not a professional medium like Andrew Jackson Davis, but she took her mediumship seriously. She made it a point to do spirit writing every morning. She often used a planchette, a heart-shaped piece of wood or plastic that is used to indicate a spirit's message by the movement on a Ouija board. The spirits who came through ranged from daughter Mary and departed friend Lilly Warner to historical figures such as Napoleon Bonaparte, who died in 1821. It is interesting to note all the conversations were recorded in radically different handwriting. One particularly interesting communication from a spirit came in new handwriting, which appeared to be rounder and and less slanted.[5]

> *Pardon, Mademoiselle, je suis—madame cannot speak French . . . What was my Josephine doing? Everything and nothing!*[6]

The communication was from Napoleon Bonaparte, who sought to use Mrs. Hooker as a medium. After her husband, John, died he took hold of her hand to write:

> *Now I feel as if I had hold of his hand, and saying dear father, this sacred spot is your mountain of transfiguration—and he say surrounded by those I loved best on earth I put off the mortal—and as I put the universal as my spirit was clothed in . . . I found that I loved the best in heaven.*[7]

Charles Beecher gives an excellent example of another amateur medium, Reverend Calvin Stowe. In his book *Spiritual Manifestation*, Beecher tells the story of his brother-in-law's visions when he was a boy. Often left without companionship, young Charles communicated with the spirit of a lad his own age for about a year. According to Stowe, "I *thought* to him and received and in return I received a silent demonstration of sympathy and fellowship from him. I called him Harvey, and used as I lay looking at his face, mentally tell him many things about the books I read, the games I played, and the childish joys and griefs I had; and in return he seem to express affection ad sympathy by a strange communication;, as lovers sometimes talk to each other by distant glances."[8] Another amazing feature of the nightly visitations was Stowe felt Harvey's hand: "I have seen H [Harvey] and felt his hand as my own."[9]

Neither Reverend Stowe nor Mrs. Hooker charged for their mediumship. Indeed, they kept their visions to themselves and only shared them with family and close friends. There are, however, those who seek fame and fortune through psychic gifts. Some mediums, such as Dr. Henry Slade, had a mixed reputation. Theosophist Madame Helena Blavatsky thought his work to be genuine, as did Professor Johann Zollner; however, members of the Sybert Commission, assembled in Pennsylvania to test mediums, claimed Slade used deception.

Henry Slade

Message to Mr. H. Richards, New Britain, Connecticut

Mr. H. Richards, New Britain, Connecticut, received a message through the mediumship of Dr. Henry Slade. What made Slade so unique was his invention of spirit slate writing. In a typical slate writing session, Slade and sitter would take their seats at a small table while grasping the corners of an ordinary slate, the type used by schoolchildren. "The slate was held under the table and all lights were extinguished. During the séance, writing sounds were heard and then a series of raps were heard at the end signalling that the message had been written. When the slate is exposed, a written message is found (usually in answer to a specific question on the part of the sitter)."[10]

Richards described his séance with Slade as follows: "The slate was placed on top of the table in plain sight, and about sixteen inches distant from the hands of any person at the table; whereat were seated out informant (H. Richards), a friend of his, and the medium. A sound of writing was plainly heard and when it ceased Mr. Slade himself lifted the slate from the table, opened, and passed it to them."[11] Mr. Richards was surprised to see that blank that he had placed on the table was now completely covered with writing. He particularly please to receive this message, which was signed by Dr. Slade's wife in spirit, Alcinda W. Slade:

> *Dear Friend, You seem to be talking about charity. I love to see a person have charity for it is one of the fruits of eternal life, and he or she who has it not in their hearts will fail of happiness either here or the world to come. He or she who loves to do good will not walk in thorny places; for those who try to do good, the divine light from heaven will shine upon them. Oh! Charity, that mighty angel, how few there be that understand its meanings. Religious dogmas are without this angel of charity for bigotry and fanatic pride are repulsive to her. We would not say we find no charity on earth, for it is not so, a bright star often shoots across the path of humanity in the form of someone who loves to seek out the lonely of earth. And if all could understand how much happiness could be gained by giving out more charity, and be governed by holy law, more light, more peace would be drawn upon earth's children. Always remember these rules, do unto others, as they should do unto you; walk in this path and you shall always find peace. I am truly your friend. A.W. Slade.*[12]

According to Richards, the spirit of Alcinda Slade wrote the message rapidly; no one touched the slate during this time. Slade had everyone at the table raise their hands to see if it would affect the writing. When the sitters raised, the writing ceased. Once the sitters at the séance table put down their hands, the spirit intelligence continued writing the message.[13]

Daniel Dunglas Home

The final example of spirit communication is a message is through the mediumship of Daniel Dunglas Home. He was the most versatile of all the Connecticut mediums. He had the ability to communicate using the planchette; through automatic writing by the influence of a spirit hand; through direct spirit—that is, writing precipitated by spirit producing audible spirit voices; and through going into a trance and allowing spirits to come through with messages.[14] The following communications were channeled through Home:

Question (Henry Jencken)—How do you make us see spirit forms?
Answer—At times we make passes over the individual to cause him to see us, sometimes we make the actual resemblance of our former clothing, and of what we were, so that we appear exactly as we were known to you on earth; sometimes we project an image that you see, sometimes we cause it to be produced upon your brain, sometimes you see us as we are, with a cloudlike aura of light around us.[15]

From "No. 25—Séance at Ashley House, October 20th."

Spiritual influence has much more to do with the affairs of the world than what you dream of. All inspiration, poetry, improvising, as in the case of the old troubadours—all that is owing to it—everything in fact, is set in motion by spiritual interference. To those who pray earnestly for and seek light and truth, light will certainly be given; our greatest difficulty is the folly of men's hearts and their blindness.[16]

FROM THE *BANNER OF LIGHT*

The *Banner of Light*, a Spiritualist newspaper, sent two representatives, Miss M.T. Shelhamer and Mrs. Paige, to a Slade séance in Boston. The séance began with the medium placing a bit of pencil between two blank slates and then setting the two slates on the left shoulder of the *Banner* representative: "At once the peculiar scratching noise with which all who have attended séance for independent writing are familiar was heard by the scribe, who inclining his head was able to catch the vibrations as the pencil moved across the interior surface of the slates; the message evidently grew longer and longer, and presently three taps indicated the end."[17]

The message was from the spirit of Mary Leahy, who said that she had passed on January 30, and she was met by her husband. She finished her slate writing with this sentiment: "If people would look more for the truth and less for fraud, they would receive more knowledge of this divine truth. The day is coming when spirits will understand the laws of control, and then they will make all believe."[18]

The above messages are as varied as the spirit communicators who spoke. Each spirit brings his or her unique style and intelligence. Most of the time, the spirits of loved ones simply wish to comfort those on this earthly plane. However, there were some who sought to enlighten as well as to demonstrate the existence of higher life. Spiritualists took great comfort from the messages they received from the enlightened spirits such as that of Mary Leahy. She encouraged those on the earthly side of life with this prediction from the other side: "The day is coming when spirits will understand the laws of control, and then they will make all believe."

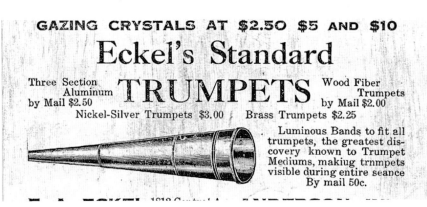

Advertisement for a standard Spiritualist trumpet. *E.A. Eckels Company, Anderson, Indiana.*

GLOSSARY

absence healing. Spiritual healing in which the healer projects positive energy from a distance.

apports. Objects that are materialized in the presence of a medium.

automatic writing, or **psychography**. The psychic ability to connect with spirits to produce written words without consciously writing. Sometimes comes from the writer passively holding a pencil on a sheet of paper or by a planchette or by Ouija board.

cabinet, or **spirit cabinets**. Portable closets in which a medium would sit for physical phenomena. Often musical instruments and a trumpet would be placed in the cabinet and the medium tied with ropes to prevent any fraudulent manipulation.

clairaudience. A form of psychic hearing in which the medium hears the voices from spirit, music or other noises from the spirit world.

clairgustience. A form of psychic smelling or tasting.

clairsentience. A form of psychic feeling in which a medium feels or senses the presence of spirit.

clairvoyance. A form of psychic seeing in which a medium will see spirit either objectively or subjectively in his or her mind's eye.

direct voice. Spirit voices that can be heard by everyone in the séance room.

ectoplasm. An organic, milky substance that is exuded by physical mediums.

levitation. The process by which an object is moved without mechanical support. People, such as medium Daniel Dunglas Home, have the ability to levitate as well.

magnetic healing. Transfer of magnetic energy or supercharged energy from one person to the other. This is usually done by laying on of hands

materialization. Appearance of spirit through formation of ectoplasm from a medium.

Ouija board. Also known as a spirit board or talking board, a flat board marked with the letters of the alphabet, the numbers zero through nine and the words *yes* and *no*.

planchette. A heart-shaped piece of wood or plastic that is used to indicate a spirit's message by the movement on a Ouija board.

precipitated paintings. Pictures that have been formed or precipitated by spirit artists.

psychic photography. The ability to capture the image of spirit on film.

psychometry. The ability to read energy by holding an object such as a watch or a ring.

séance. A sitting that is held by a medium to communicate with the dead.

slate writing. The practice of spirit writing messages on slates. Usually two chalkboards are bound together with a small piece of chalk in the middle. At the close of the séance, the slates would be opened to reveal messages written by spirits.

spirit. A discarnate being that exists in an invisible realm.

table tipping. Communication from spirit by means of spirit raps on a table.

trumpets, or **spirit trumpets**. Speaking tubes that were said to magnify the whispered voices of spirits to audible range. Early Spiritualists used copper trumpets. Modern mediums favor lightweight aluminum trumpets.

NOTES

CHAPTER 1

1. Mishlove, *Roots of Consciousness*, 41.
2. fst.org/spirit3.htm.
3. geohanover.com/docs/fox2.htm.
4. Ibid.
5. Ibid.
6. Melton, "Richmond, Cora Scott (1840–1923)," in *The Encyclopedia of Religious Phenomena*, 269.
7. en.wikipedia.org/wiki/Cora_L._V._Scott.
8. Barrett, "Introduction," *Life Work of Cora L. V. Scott Richmond*.
9. Crowell, *Identity of Primitive Christianity*, 339.
10. prairieghosts.com/eddy.html.
11. Taylor, *Ghosts By Gaslight*, 70.
12. Hoover, *Philadelphia Spiritualism*, 85.
13. survivalafterdeath.info/mediums/holmes-nelson.htm.
14. en.wikipedia.org/wiki/Society for Psychical Research.
15. Mann, *Follies and Frauds*, 40–41.
16. Von Schrenck-Notzing, "Imposture of Pseudo Medium Ladislas Lasslo," 105–34.

CHAPTER 2

1. nsac.org/LilyDale.php.
2. spirithistory.iapsop.com/spiritualists_petition_to_congress.html.

3. Doyle, *History of Spiritualism*, 89–111.
4. nsac.org/LilyDale.php.
5. spirithistory.iapsop.com/spiritualists_petition_to_congress.htm.
6. Chambers, *Victor Hugo's Conversations with the Spirit World*.
7. mysteriousplanchette.com/Manu_Portal/hudsontuttle.html.
8. damnedct.com/phelps-mansion-stratford#sthash.Et4jsDYh.dpu.
9. prairieghosts.com/stratford.html.
10. Ibid.
11. twainquotes.com/18660204t.html.

CHAPTER 3

1. Davis, *Magic Staff*, 263.
2. fst.org/spirit3.htm.
3. Ibid.
4. cassadaga.org/ajdavis.htm.
5. Brown, *Heyday of Spiritualism*, 29.
6. Ibid., 90.
7. Ibid., 91.
8. Steiger and Steiger, *Gale Encyclopedia of the Unusual and Unexplained*.
9. Brown, *Heyday of Spiritualism*, 93–94.
10. Ibid.
11. Davis and Fishbough, *Principles of Nature*, 62.
12. seekeronline.info/journals/y2007/jun07.html.
13. andrewjacksondavis.com/article1.htm.
14. Brown, *Heyday of Spiritualism*, 108.
15. survivalafterdeath.info/library/fodor/chapter8.htm.
16. andrewjacksondavis.com/article1.htm.

CHAPTER 4

1. people.wcsu.edu/lupoli001/phelps.htm.
2. stratfordstar.com/29009/the-stratford-witch-trial-of-goody-bassett.
3. prairieghosts.com/stratford.html.
4. damnedct.com/phelps-mansion-stratford.
5. Beecher, *Spiritual Manifestations*, 20.
6. prairieghosts.com/stratford.html.
7. Beecher, *Spiritual Manifestations*, 21.
8. Ibid., 21.
9. Ibid., 22.
10. prairieghosts.com/stratford.html.

11. Brown, *Heyday of Spiritualism*, 149–50.
12. andrewjacksondavis.com/article4.htm.
13. prairieghosts.com/stratford.html.
14. Brown, *Heyday of Spiritualism*, 155.

CHAPTER 5

1. Doyle, *History of Spiritualism*, 196–97.
2. Lamont, *First Psychic*, 5.
3. Ibid., 14–15.
4. psychictruth.info/Medium_Daniel_Dunglas_Home.htm.
5. mysteriousuniverse.org/2014/02/levitating-home-the-odd-spiritualism-of-daniel-dunglas-homes.
6. Lamont, *First Psychic*, 28–29.
7. seteantigoshepta.blogspot.com/2009/08/daniel-douglas-home-paranormal-mais.html.
8. reference.com/browse/daniel+dunglas.
9. Home, *D.D. Home*, 32.
10. survivalafterdeath.info/articles/podmore/index.htm.
11. Haase, *Een Vreemdelinge in Den Haag*.
12. psychictruth.info/Medium_Daniel_Dunglas_Home.htm.
13. Ibid.
14. Podmore, *Mediums of the 19th Century*, 254.
15. Beckley, *Revealing the Bizarre Powers of Harry Houdini*, 225.
16. Ibid.
17. unexplainedstuff.com/Mediums-and-Mystics/Mediums-and-Channelers-Daniel-dunglas-home-1833-1886.html.
18. Crookes, "Notes of Séances with D.D. Home," 107–8, 116.

CHAPTER 6

1. Newton, *Modern Bethesda*, 76.
2. Willis, *Mark and Livy*, 25.
3. wrf.org/men-women-medicine/dr-james-newton-healing-gift.php.
4. Newton, *Modern Bethesda*, 76.
5. wrf.org/men-women-medicine/dr-james-newton-healing-gift.php.
6. Ibid.
7. Newton, *Modern Bethesda*, 78.
8. Ibid., 84.
9. Ibid.

10. Ibid.
11. Ibid., 78.
12. Ibid., 82.
13. Ibid., 80.
14. Ibid., 92–96.
15. wrf.org/men-women-medicine/dr-james-newton-healing-gift.php.
16. Newton, *Modern Bethesda*, 85.
17. Ibid., 82.
18. Ibid., 83.
19. Ibid., 88–91.
20. Ibid., 83.
21. Ibid., 202.
22. Ibid.

Chapter 7

1. brainyquote.com/quotes/quotes/h/harrietbee383022.html.
2. harrietbeecherstowe.org.
3. Ibid.
4. en.wikipedia.org/wiki/Harriet_Beecher_Stowe.
5. google.com/?gws_rd=ssl#q=Children+s+death%2C+Victorian+times.
6. Koester, *Harriet Beecher Stowe*, 220.
7. Ibid.
8. Ibid, 229.
9. Beecher, *Spiritual Manifestations*, 30.
10. Ibid., 33.
11. Ibid., 34.
12. Harriet Beecher Stowe letter to George Elliot, February 8, 1872, New York Public Library.
13. Koester, *Harriet Beecher Stowe*, 296.
14. Ibid.
15. Ibid., 297.
16. Ibid., 298.
17. Ibid., 299.
18. en.wikipedia.org/wiki/Harriet_Beecher_Stowe.

Chapter 8

1. Maynard, *Lincoln a Spiritualist?*, 64–68.
2. Ibid., 9.
3. Maynard, *Séances in Washington*, 16.

4. Ibid., 15.
5. Maynard, *Lincoln a Spiritualist?*, 16.
6. Ibid.
7. Ibid., 31.
8. Ibid.
9. Ibid., 31–32.
10. scandalouswoman.blogspot.com/2013/12/guest-blogger-michelle-hamilton-on.html.
11. Ibid.
12. Maynard, *Lincoln a Spiritualist?*, 69–73.
13. Ibid., 68.
14. scandalouswoman.blogspot.com/2013/12/guest-blogger-michelle-hamilton-on.html.
15. Ibid.
16. https://kindle.amazon.com/work/spiritualist-memories-president-introduction-pendleton.

CHAPTER 9

1. Andrew, *Nook Farm*, 57.
2. Ibid., 56.
3. Ibid., 57.
4. Campbell, *Tempest Tossed*, 135.
5. Sinclair, *Modern Hydrotherapy*, 13.
6. Ibid.
7. Campbell, *Tempest Tossed*, 133.
8. Ibid., 116.
9. Marryat, *There Is No Death*, 220–27.
10. Andrew, *Nook Farm*, 56.
11. Ibid., 58–59.
12. Ibid., 60–61.
13. Ibid., 57–58.
14. Campbell, *Tempest Tossed*, 133.
15. Ibid., 149.
16. Ibid.
17. Ibid.
18. Andrew, *Nook Farm*, 223.
19. Campbell, *Tempest Tossed*, 175.
20. Schreiner, *Passionate Beechers*, 353.
21. Campbell, *Tempest Tossed*, 176.
22. Ibid., 177.

Chapter **10**

1. Havelin, *Victoria Woodhull*, 15.
2. Goldsmith, *Other Powers*, 63.
3. Havelin, *Victoria Woodhull*, 13.
4. Ibid., 27–29.
5. Goldsmith, *Other Powers*, 108.
6. Ibid., 65.
7. victoria-woodhull.com/tiltonbio.htm.
8. eloquentwoman.blogspot.com/2013/09/famous-speech-friday-victoria-woodhulls.html.
9. brainyquote.com/quotes/authors/v/victoria_woodhull.html.
10. wikipedia.org/wiki/Victoria_Woodhull.
11. victoria-woodhull.com/faq.htm.

Chapter **11**

1. Clemens, *Mark Twain, His Life and Work*.
2. quinnipiac.edu/media/abl/etext/hartford/hartford.html.
3. marktwainhouse.org/house/history.php.
4. troytaylorbooks.blogspot.com/2014/11/mark-twain-and-supernatural.html?
5. twainquotes.com/18660204at.html.
6. Twain, *Mark Twain's Letters*, 48–50.
7. Twain, *Autobiography*, 274.
8. Ibid.
9. Willis, *Mark and Livy*, 25.
10. Campbell, *Tempest Tossed*, 148.
11. connecticutmag.com/Blog/History/March-2014/Tempest-Tossed-The-Spirit-of-Isabella-Beecher-Hooker.
12. Twain, "Schoolhouse Hill," *Huck Finn and Tom Sawyer*, 245.
13. Steve Courtney, *We Shall Have Them with Us Always*, 80.

Chapter **12**

1. Beecher, *Spiritual Manifestations*, 38.
2. Ibid., 9.
3. Ibid., 13.
4. Ibid., 14.
5. Ibid., 15.
6. Ibid., 16.
7. Ibid., 21.

8. Ibid.
9. Ibid., 23.
10. prairieghosts.com/stratford.html.
11. Beecher, *Spiritual Manifestations*, 23.
12. Ibid., 29.
13. Ibid., 31.
14. Ibid., 50–51.
15. Ibid., 266.
16. Ibid.
17. *Holy Bible*, King James Version, Matthew 17:1–5.
18. Brittan, *Review of Rev. Charles Beecher's Report*, 42–43.
19. Ibid., 69.
20. Ibid., 78.

CHAPTER 13

1. Katz, *Dearest Genius*, 3.
2. Ibid., 40.
3. Ibid., 63.
4. Ibid., 66.
5. Ibid., 44.
6. en.wikipedia.org/wiki/Leonora_Piper.
7. en.wikipedia.org/wiki/Society_for_Psychical_Research2301.
8. rmslusitania.info/people/saloon/edwin-friend.
9. Ibid.
10. Cunningham, *My Godmother, Theodate Pope Riddle*, 63.
11. Ibid.
12. *Hartford Courant*, "Nothing Unusual About the Messages of Prof. Friend," October 18, 1915.
13. Fenn, *My Godmother, Theodate Pope Riddle*, 77.
14. Ibid.

CHAPTER 14

1. spirithistory.iapsop.com/1861_spiritualist_register.html.
2. spirithistory.iapsop.com/1880_professional_spiritualists.html.
3. eastlymehistoricalsociety.org/index_files/Page1315.htm.
4. Nettie Pease Fox, "Camp Meetings," *Spiritual Scientist*, 376.
5. Mike Caro, "Spiritualist Camp Ends Season," *Hartford Courant*, September 6, 1977.

6. *Hartford Courant,* "Beneath Niantic's Pines: Pleasant Days at Spiritualist Camp Grounds," August 17, 1894.
7. Ibid.
8. *Hartford Courant,* "Spiritualist Meet: Annual Sessions of Connecticut Association," May 6, 1901, 8.
9. Ibid.
10. *Hartford Courant,* "Spirits Come for Various Message," May 8, 1916.
11. Ibid.
12. *Hartford Courant,* "Connecticut Spiritualist Association Meets," August 28, 1921.
13. *Hartford Courant,* "Settlements Take Separate Paths: East Lyme," February 7, 1978.
14. Lawrence C. Nizza, "Journey into the Spirit World," *Hartford Courant,* September 8, 1957.
15. *Hartford Courant,* "Spiritualists Start Their Annual Session Here," May 4, 1930.
16. *Day,* "East Lyme," June 16, 1980.
17. Ibid.

EPILOGUE

1 Davis, *Great Harmonia,* 10.
2. psychictruth.info/Medium_Andrew_Jackson_Davis.htm.
3. Ibid.
4. Ibid.
5. Campbell, *Tempest Tossed,* 170.
6. Ibid., 173.
7. Beecher, *Spiritual Manifestations,* 40.
8. Ibid., 41.
9. en.wikipedia.org/wiki/Society for Psychical Research.
10. archive.randi.org/site/index.php/swift-blog/1325-the-amazing-henry-slade.html.
11. Nagy, *Spirit Writing,* 98.
12. Ibid., 98–99.
13. Ibid., 101–2.
14. Adare, *Experiences in Spiritualism with Mr. D.D. Home.*
15. Ibid.
16. Ibid.
17. Nagy, *Spirit Writing,* 101.
18. Ibid., 101–2.

BIBLIOGRAPHY

Adare, Lord. *Experiences in Spiritualism with Mr. D.D. Home*. London: Thomas Scott, 1869.

Andrew, Kenneth R. *Nook Farm: Mark Twain's Hartford Circle*. Seattle: University of Washington Press, 1950.

Barrett, H.D. *The Life Work of Cora L.V. Scott Richmond*. 2nd ed. Chicago: National Spiritualist Association of Churches, 1991.

Beckley, Timothy Green. *Revealing the Bizarre Powers of Harry Houdini*. New Brunswick, NJ: Global Communications, 2014.

Beecher, Charles. *Spiritual Manifestations*. London: Forgotten Books, 2013. First published 1879 by Lee and Shephard Publishers.

Braude, Ann. *Radical Spirits*. Bloomington: Indiana University Press, 2001.

Brittan, B.B. *A Review of Rev. Charles Beecher's Report Concerning Spiritual Manifestations*. London: Forgotten Books, 2012.

Brown, Slater. *The Heyday of Spiritualism*. New York: Pocket Books Edition, 1972.

Campbell, Susan. *Tempest Tossed: The Spirit of Isabella Hooker*. Middletown: CT: Wesleyan University Press, 2014.

Chambers, John. *Victor Hugo's Conversations with the Spirit World*, Rochester, VT: Destiny Press, 2008.

Clemens, William Montgomery. *Mark Twain, His Life and Work*. San Francisco, CA: Clemens Publishing Company, 1892.

Courtney, Steve. *We Shall Have Them with Us Always*. Hartford, CT: Mark Twain House and Museum, 2013.

Crowell, Eugene. *The Identity of Primitive Christianity and Modern Spiritualism*. New York: G.W. Carleton & Company, 1874–75.

Cunningham, Phyllis Fenn. *My Godmother, Theodate Pope Riddle*. Canaan, NH: Phoenix Publishing, 1983.

Davis, Andrew Jackson. *The Great Harmonia*. Boston, MA: B. Marsh, 1850.

———. *The Magic Staff*. New York: J.S. Brown & Company, 1857.

Davis, Andrew Jackson, and William Fishbough. *Principles of Nature*. London: John Chapman, 1847.

DeSalvo, John. *Andrew Jackson Davis*. Lulu.com, 2005.

Doyle, Arthur Conan. *The History of Spiritualism*. London: Cassell & Company Ltd., 1926.

Goldsmith, Barbara. *Other Powers*. New York: Alfred A. Knopf, 1998.

Haasse, Hella S. *Een Vreemdelinge in Den Hag*. Amsterdam: Sijthoff, 1988.

Havelin, Kate. *Victoria Woodhull*. Minneapolis, MN: Twenty-First Century Books, 2007.

Hedrick, Joan D. *Harriet Beecher Stowe*. New York: Oxford University Press, 1989.

Home, Julie de Gloumeline. *D.D. Home: His Life and Mission*. London: Trubner & Company, 1888.

Hoover, Stephanie. *Philadelphia Spiritualism and the Curious Case of Katie King*. Charleston, SC: The History Press, 2013.

Katz, Sandra L. *Dearest Genius*. Windsor, CT: Tidemark Press, 2005.

Koester, Nancy. *Harriet Beecher Stowe: A Spiritual Life*. Grand Rapids, MI: William B. Eerdmans Publishing Company, 2014.

Lamont, Peter. *The First Psychic*. London: Little, Brown, 2005.

Mann, Walter. *The Follies and Frauds of Spiritualism*. London: Watts & Company, 1919.

Marryat, Florence. *There Is No Death*. New York: Causeway Books, 1978.

Maynard, Nettie Colbun. *Séances in Washington*. Toronto, ON: Ancient Wisdom Publishing, 2009.

———. *Was Abraham Lincoln a Spiritualist?* Philadelphia, PA: Rufus C. Hartranft, 1891.

Melton, J. Gordon. *The Encyclopedia of Religious Phenomena*. Detroit, MI: Visible Ink Press, 2008.

Mishlove, Jeffery. *Roots of Consciousness*. Tulsa, OK: Council Oak Books, 1979.

Nagy, Ron. *Spirit Writing*. Lakeville, MN: Galde Press, 2008.

Newton, J.R. *The Modern Bethesda*. N.p.: Newton Publishing Company, 1879.

Owen, Alex. *The Darkened Room*. Chicago: University of Chicago Press, 1989.

Podmore, Frank. *Mediums of the 19th Century*. Whitefish, MT: Kessinger Publishing, 2003.

Schreiner, Samuel A., Jr. *The Passionate Beechers*. Hoboken, NJ: John Wiley and Sons, 2003.

Sinclair, Marybetts. *Modern Hydrotherapy for the Massage Therapist*. Philadelphia, PA: Lippincott, Williams & Wilkins, 2007.

Steiger, Brad, and Sherry Hansen Steiger. *The Gale Encyclopedia of the Unusual and Unexplained*. Detroit, MI: Thomson/Gale, 2003.

Taylor, Troy. *Ghosts by Gaslight*. Decatur, IL: Whitechapel Productions Press, 2007.

Twain, Mark. *Huck Finn and Tom Sawyer Among the Indians and Other Unfinished Stories*. Berkeley: University of California Press, 1989.

Twain, Mark, and Charles Neider. *The Autobiography of Mark Twain*. New York: Harper & Brothers, 1959.

Twain, Mark, and Albert Bigelow Paine. *Mark Twain's Letters*. New York: Harper & Brothers, 1917.

Van Why, Joseph. *Nook Farm*. Hartford, CT: Stowe-Day Foundation, 1975.

Von Schrenck-Notzing, A.F. "The Imposture of Pseudo Medium Ladislas Lasslo (Imitation of Materialization Phenomena)." *Revue Métapsychique*, no. 2 (1924): 105–34.

White, Barbara. *The Beecher Sisters*. New Haven, CT: Yale University Press, 2003.

Willis, Resa. *Mark and Livy: The Love Story of Mark Twain and the Woman Who Almost Tamed Him*. Abingdon, OX: Taylor & Francis, 2003.

Wilson, Forrest. *Crusader in Crinoline*. New York: L.P. Lippincott Company, 1941.

INDEX

ABOUT THE AUTHOR

E laine Kuzmeskus, MS, director of the New England School of Metaphysics, is the author of seven books on the occult, including *Connecticut Ghosts, The Art of Mediumship* and *The Medium Who Baffled Houdini*. She has also written articles for *Fate* magazine and the *American Federation of Astrologers*. Recently, she was featured on *Better Connecticut* and the **PBS** special *Things That Go Bump in the Night*. During the last twenty years, she has been a presenter at the Learning Annex in New York City, Lily Dale Assembly in New York and colleges throughout New England. She is also a nationally recognized Spiritualist medium. In 1997, she was selected to conduct the Official Houdini Séance. Elaine enjoys hearing from readers, so feel free to contact her on her website, www.theartofmediumship.com.

Elaine M. Kuzmeskus. *Moto Photo, Enfield, Connecticut.*